Finding the River

The Energy Self-Help Manual
For Surviving Life's Challenges

Sally Topham

Finding the River

The energy self-help manual for surviving life's challenges

© 2010 Sally Topham

ISBN 1-873483-16-3

First Edition

Published by

DragonRising Publishing

The Starfields Network Ltd.

45 Gildredge Road

Eastbourne

East Sussex

BN21 4RY

United Kingdom

www.DragonRising.com

Printed and bound in Great Britain by
CPI Antony Rowe, Chippenham and Eastbourne

Cover illustration, book design, and book comp and illustrations by Sheryl Tongue,
www.stonehillgraphics.com

Finding the River

The Energy Self-Help Manual
For Surviving Life's Challenges

This book is dedicated to
Juliane Koepke
whose courage and tenacity has been such an inspiration

Contents

List of Exercises

List of Figures

Foreword

Are you peaceful and fulfilled right here, right now? Without consulting your mind for an answer, take a couple of long, slow, deep breaths and notice how your body is responding to the question. Focus only on the question. Let your body and its sensations provide the answer.

What are you experiencing—a sense of well-being and expansion or tension, contraction, heaviness or tightness? Regardless of what your mind might say and as extraordinary as this might sound, our bodies are able to communicate the truth in the moment more accurately than the mind. There are some exceptions, but in my ten years of working with, what I refer to as body wisdom, I have found this to be true. Indeed I will go one step further and say this: When it comes to deep emotional healing and personal growth, my experience has been that positive lasting shifts in mind and consciousness are often easier to bring about by working with our body than with the mind. Our bodies speak the truth and our bodies can be a portal into truth.

Regardless of what truth your body spoke in relation to the question above, you can experience peace and fulfilment right now. Are you sceptical? Do you believe me? Let's put it to the test. Ask the question again, notice what you are feeling. Now embrace and welcome those bodily sensations with the same energy and warmth that you would cuddle a newly born baby. If the baby image doesn't evoke warmth within you, choose something that does! Now breathe into the centre of the strongest body sensation and as you do so silently say to that sensation, "I am really pleased you are here." Keep breathing into the sensation and as you do so notice the spaciousness that is starting to open up in its centre. You can't make it happen—it's a case of allowing it to happen and it will, as long as you are able to stay present, hold focus and breathe. If you get distracted, frustrated or caught up in a story of "its not working", just smile to yourself and return your attention to your breath and to the centre of the strongest bodily sensation. Once you become aware of a spaciousness emerging, allow yourself to be pulled as though by a tractor beam towards and into this space. Keep going until you feel both peaceful and expansive. You might even feel blissful. The whole process takes as long it needs to take (usually between 5 and 30 minutes). If you do this, and I really encourage you to do it, you will discover something quite profound. In any given moment your relationship to "what is", in this case your body's sensations, is the determinant of whether you will experience a sense of peace and fulfilment or not. By resisting or fighting "what is", you suffer; by embracing and welcoming "what is", you experience peace. This is not just some fanciful esoteric promise, but a reality that you can discover for yourself with this experiment.

Why is this so? Why does surrendering to "space" shift the quality of our inner experience? It's because our true nature is the spacious awareness within which the content of our life experience is arising. You are the peace and joy that you seek. These qualities of experience rest not in the future or in fantasy or in our thoughts, but in the here and now.

The author of this book, Sally Topham, understands this. She has done a wonderful job of sharing the tools and approaches that have helped her along her own path of health, healing and awakening into present moment awareness. If you choose to follow her advice—and I recommend you do—you won't just learn how to improve your health or heal emotionally, you will discover your own unique path into the flow of life. I wish you the best. Enjoy the journey.

Dr Mark Atkinson MBBS BSc (HONS) FRSPH FBSIM

Dr Atkinson is a holistic medical doctor, well-being expert, author of *The Mind–Body Bible* and developer of human potential coaching. His website is www.DrMarkAtkinson.com.

Acknowledgements
and Permissions

I've encountered many teachers throughout my journey—some of whom I've met and worked with, some whose teachings I've read and absorbed, and some wise ones who are animals or who've appeared to me in meditation. In addition, I'm fortunate in having had some wonderful friends who've given me the benefit of their advice, guidance, support and encouragement through the years. The friends, authors, teachers and guides whose names you see below have been especially helpful and inspirational on many levels. Without them I never would have travelled very far along my path. Much gratitude and appreciation to them all.

Josef Alberts, Meher Baba, Shyamji Bhatnager, William Bloom, Judy Byrne, Julia Cameron, Patricia Carrington, Annette Carson, Deepak Chopra, Upen Choksi, Gary Craig, Ram Dass, Lucie Davidson, Wayne Dyer, Donna Eden, Julia Edge, Ezekiel, David Feinstein, Ganesh, Kahlil Gibran, Ian Gordon-Brown, Gospel of the Essences, G. I .Gurdjieff, Gurumai, Andrew Harvey, Silvia Hartmann, Esther and Jerry Hicks, Sandra Hillawi, Melanie Hoffstead, Paula Horan, Mary Huber, I Ching, Jak, Ani Jinpa, Carl Jung, Leslie Kenton, Madison King, Karen Kingston, Jack Kornfield, Elizabeth Kubler-Ross, Dalai Lama, Pam Lidford, Denise Linn, Christine Longakre, Carol Look, Richard Mark, Lynne McTaggart, Mother Meera, Sandy Montague, Baba Mukhtananda, Caroline Myss, Lindsay Nash, OMS Group, Othar, Candace Pert, Michael Pope, Ernest Rossi, Carol and Chris Rudd, Howard Sasportas, Franklyn Sills, Kajal Sheth, Charan Singh, Sophie, Dr Randolph Stone, Barbara Summers, Hawayo Takata, Dr Mikao Usui, Woolfie, Roger Woolgar, and Zoaren.

•

Special thanks and gratitude also to the following people who have given me permission to use some of their material in this book:

William Bloom, Donna Eden and David Feinstein,
Silvia Hartmann, Andrew Harvey and Ernest Rossi

Prologue

The Story Behind the Title

It all began on Christmas Eve, 1971, when I saw the evening newspaper headlines about an air disaster in Peru. A passenger plane on an internal flight between Lima and Pucallpa had unaccountably exploded in mid air and fallen to earth in the dense Amazonian jungle. All 94 people on board were feared dead.

I was saddened to hear about this tragedy and found myself pondering that there was so often a disaster somewhere in the world at Christmas time. Were these catastrophes really visited upon us by Cosmic/Universal/Heavenly forces as some people might think? I found it hard to believe that a vengeful God was punishing hapless scapegoats for the misdeeds of humanity. It seemed more likely that they were some kind of a wake-up call for us. Surely they could be more realistically interpreted as an opportunity to re-evaluate our lives so that we might perhaps learn to live more in the moment, to enjoy life, to have more awareness and gratitude? I dwelt upon these thoughts, but, unsurprisingly, came to no conclusions. As I wrapped up the last of the Christmas presents, I was simply left with a slightly uncomfortable feeling that there might be something here for me to learn, although I had absolutely no idea what it could be.

Media focus on the disaster melted away over the ensuing days. However, just after New Year, the tragedy was suddenly brought back to world attention. Reports started appearing in the news that, against all the odds, a seventeen-year-old German girl, Juliane Koepke, who had been a passenger on that plane, had survived. The world was agog with details of her miraculous escape and survival.

Juliane had been travelling with her mother (a famous ornithologist) from the Peruvian capital of Lima to spend Christmas with her father (a biologist) in Pucallpa, a city in the eastern part of the country. The plane was struck by lightening, burst into flames and Juliane was ejected, still in her seat, into a tree miles below that cushioned her fall. Miraculously, she suffered only a broken collarbone, a gash to her right arm and the loss of vision in one eye. She also found she only had one shoe.

Knowing she would surely die unless she found a way out of the disaster area, Juliane resolved to use botanical knowledge and survival skills she had learned from her father to find her way through the jungle and back to civilisation and help. Armed only with a stout stick and a bag of toffees found in the wreckage, she set forth. Remembering that her first requirement was to find land that sloped downhill, because this would lead to a stream, she looked for plants that grew beside water. In this way Nature guided her to a nearby stream that provided her with a source of clean drinking water. She knew if she followed the course of the stream it would eventually lead her to a river, and once she had found the river she would find areas of civilisation and be able to seek help.

Juliane's incredible and courageous trek for survival through the inhospitable Amazonian jungle took her ten days. During this time she was bitten and stung mercilessly by insects and bruised and battered by having to force her way through dense undergrowth. The stream she had been following ultimately led her to the River Amazon where she eventually came to a hut used by lumbermen who worked on the great waterway. When the lumbermen found her, she was lying in a canoe moored nearby where, exhausted and sick, she had finally collapsed. After a seven-hour canoe trip to the nearest village, help was summoned and Juliane was flown to Pucallpa Hospital where she made a complete recovery and was reunited with her distraught father.

I became totally obsessed with this story and probably read every paper that ran accounts of the epic tale, marvelling all the time at the courage of this young girl. Her heroism spoke to a place deep within me that was desperately seeking help and finding none. At that time in my life, I was feeling rather lost and vulnerable and was finding no support in the areas where I sought it—boyfriends who were unable to be present emotionally and a family that was unforthcoming in its encouragement of my dreams and ambitions. Furthermore, my career in the theatre caused me a lot of stress and I had become far too reliant on cigarettes and alcohol as a means of coping.

In 1971, it was a time when many of the hippie values and philosophies of the 1960s were starting to become absorbed into general living. I was one of the generation who had been caught up in the social, cultural and artistic revolution that had begun. As an Aquarian, I had happily bought into ideas about expanding consciousness, spirituality, healing, meditation and new ways of being. I was excited by the general sense of opening, expansion, liberation and flow. The only trouble was that I couldn't find a way of getting into any of it. I merely stuck my toes in the water from time to time and engaged at rather superficial levels. The truth was that, deep down inside, even though I was feeling very stuck and blocked and was desperately seeking change, a large part of me was terrified of stepping out into the unknown.

I think Juliane's traumatic experience and miraculous escape had an almost mythic quality to it that I found inspirational. It was a metaphor for moving out of the darkness and into the light. In the months that followed, I resolved that I too wanted to develop a tenacity that would see me through challenges and difficulties. Above all, I knew beyond a shadow of doubt that I wanted to get out of this feeling of being stuck and dive into this wonderful flow of New Age consciousness.

As I started focussing on what I really wanted and believing it was possible to find it, so those things were drawn towards me. Before long, I had met a friend of a friend who spoke with great enthusiasm about a personal development group he had discovered. He persuaded me to go to some meetings and, to my delight, it appeared to be exactly what I'd been looking for. The teachings were a blend of the esoteric woven in with meditations and healing techniques and a strong emphasis towards connecting with nature. I couldn't wait to begin! Once I'd committed to the group, I was totally involved in the work. I later realised this was an incredibly important stepping stone into the rest of my life.

In time I left this particular group and moved on to other areas of interest. As the years rolled by and I journeyed further along my path of self discovery, the memory of that young German girl often came to mind. The many streams I've followed have led me through my own personal jungles and I'm still travelling! I've sat at the feet of Indian gurus and other charismatic teachers, read countless books by renowned writers on personal and spiritual development, and attended numerous courses, workshops and lectures by respected teachers on the subject of healing and energy. Along the way, I also placed myself in the hands of several therapists of various persuasions in an effort to find ways through my extremely tangled emotional undergrowth!

Eventually I became a teacher and a therapist myself. As I worked with my clients and students the germ of an idea began to seed within me. I started to ponder on the possibility of making a compilation of the techniques, healings and exercises that had helped me emerge from a feeling of loss and isolation into one of connection and flow. This was when the title, *Finding the River*, first floated into my mind. I knew the name was 100% right but I couldn't decide how to format the idea. It wasn't until the spring of 2008 that I realised this project, that had been composting for so long, could be made into a self-help book with that title. A couple of months later, the chance to write this book for DragonRising Publications arose.

So here it is. My book doesn't focus on just one method of self-help, for experience has shown me that we need to explore many different ways of helping ourselves. As we seek out the possibilities, so we begin to discover which particular techniques and concepts blend together in a synthesis that works best for us as individuals. In this way, we gradually move towards a sense of flow within ourselves. The journey towards the river is about learning to care for, nurture and heal yourself. About finding your centre, opening your heart, learning to feel joy and abundance and finding the peace and tranquillity within. It's about planting new seeds in your life, watching them flower and reaping the harvest of your efforts. Above all, it's about understanding your connection with Nature and learning to flow with its boundless energy and wisdom.

I wish you much joy in finding your river.

Sally

Part I

Body, Mind, and Spirit

Chapter 1

Tuning in and Feeling the Connection

L ife is like a river. We navigate the rapids with the challenges we face. We overflow with emotions when we feel sad and hurt or happy and joyful. We can recede or dry up when we feel threatened and unsafe or blocked and negative. We flow when we open our hearts and allow love, understanding and compassion to rise up within us. The high tides are when we experience abundance and fulfilment and the low tides are when we feel defeated or at a loss. Every bend in the river is a reflection of the cycles and changes we experience.

I've been in all of these places myself. And I want to share with you some of the methods and techniques I've learnt and used to help myself and my clients through the ups and downs we all have to face. Everything offered in this book is based on two fundamental things: first, that there are many ways of helping yourself through all kinds of problems, and second the importance of learning to keep our energies free and flowing.

I'm going to be telling you about lots of things you can do to help yourself find and maintain a better state of inner balance, all of which will be a foundation for finding your personal river. I'm going to be giving you core strategies to help you hack your way through the undergrowth and get you out of the jungle! I'll be describing various aspects of energy work and teaching you some techniques you can use. I'm also going to be explaining how working in harmony with the cycles of Nature can help you in this process.

I'm not going to promise that you will magically heal every part of your life or that you will be able to let go of all the unskilful bits of you which get in the way of becoming who you really are. I'm afraid there aren't any quick fixes in this kind of work. But what I can promise is that by following these methods and guidelines, you can make life a whole lot easier for yourself! By using these ideas, you can have less stress, more ability to cope and, if you use them regularly and on an ongoing basis, you will find you're gradually growing more in tune with your true self.

Your way forward starts from the moment you decide that you want to change. So, let's begin!

Have you ever found that if you have a problem and you go out for a walk in nature, something seems to shift in you for the better? Somehow, your state of mind is improved? You may not have actually solved your problem, but by some means or another, you've managed to put some space around it? Taking your problems for a walk can be very helpful!

Now, just in case you want to tell me that you lead a busy life and don't have the time to go out for lovely country walks to clear your mind when things are difficult, let me assure you that you don't have to live in the country in order to do this. You don't have to have a garden either. Neither of those things is necessary in order to connect with nature. You could just have a window box or a potted plant in your living room or a bunch of flowers on the table! And if you don't have any of these things, you could simply tear a picture of a beautiful view out of a magazine and stick it on your wall and spend a bit of time enjoying looking at it! All of these methods are fine if you can use them. But if all else fails, the quickest and easiest way of connecting with nature is through your imagination!

We all hold images in our minds. We're like a camcorder that's constantly in operation. We shoot the film with our eyes and re-run the scenes in our imagination. And every time we do that, we are *right there* again, re-experiencing everything we felt!

Before you go any further, I'd like to invite you to do Exercise 1.

Exercise 1: The Magic of Memory and Imagination

Just take a moment to fastback through your library of mental images and choose a time when you've been out in Nature and it felt really good. You could go back to a childhood memory if you like, or stick with a more recent recollection. Maybe you were walking by the sea, or sitting looking at a sunset, or it could have been when you were on holiday in another country.

I'd like you to select one of these memories right now. Make a quick decision about which one you want to recall. When you've decided, I'd like you to close your eyes, just go inside and bring the image of that place back into your mind.

Imagine the place. Remember the weather. Is it warm or cold or somewhere in-between? Imagine the sounds. What are the sights you can see? Can you smell anything which was very particular to that place? How does it feel being there? Allow all those sensations to come back to you.

Do this now. Don't read on until you've done it. Stay there for as long as you want. Then come back and open your eyes.

How was that? Most people can quite easily re-experience what they felt by using image recall. By the way, notice where in your body you felt those good feelings and what they were like. For example, if you felt a sense of somehow opening up and feeling more spacious inside did you feel it in your head or your chest or your belly? Or somewhere else? Just make a mental note of where it was for your own information and we'll come back to that in a later chapter.

If you're able to re-experience that nice feeling without even being there, it's as good as having a magic carpet, isn't it? Imagination is wonderful in this respect. It can transport you instantly to any place or time you choose. So next time you're wrestling with a problem and you aren't able to physically take it for a walk, all you've got to do is repeat that little exercise. Only this time, try to stay a bit longer and be very conscious of allowing yourself to soak up all that nice healing space you're remembering and let it flood through you.

Using your imagination to take you to a place inside where you can retreat and feel safe and good is a very healing thing to do for yourself. This way of working is totally natural for us because we've been using our imaginations since we were children. We've got a whole host of film clips which we store in our minds, and we can re-create these images for ourselves whenever we want, wherever we are, and at any time of the day or night.

Exercise 2 will help you create that safe place within yourself.

Exercise 2: Creating a Safe Place Within Yourself

You might like to refine Exercise 1 by deciding which, of all your memories, is the very best one you ever experienced in Nature. Have fun scrolling through your memories. Then use the "film clip" of that image, and, just as you did in Exercise 1, go back and enjoy that glorious space. Let it become a special, safe and healing place where you can retreat whenever things get too much. It's a simple, easy thing to do and you can help yourself enormously by summoning that memory.

Try doing this before you go to sleep tonight. It doesn't matter if you fall asleep in the middle of it. It's a very nice place to fall asleep in! You may find that doing this exercise gives you a particularly good night's sleep and the next day, you wake up feeling more refreshed than usual.

Do this exercise whenever you need it.

Before I continue, let's try to understand what may be happening to us when we go out into the countryside or into a local park or even into our own back garden. Nature is quiet and often full of wide open spaces. Just being there and soaking it up helps you to find space in yourself. You see, when you get yourself into a frazzled state of one sort or another, your energy and your body tends to contract, and sometimes your mind seizes up to the point where it can feel absolutely solid. Nature diffuses this by filling you with a sense of expansion, which is why it can make you feel better, clearer and more relaxed.

And don't we all need that?

Sadly, in our present culture, we're so engrossed in our busy lives that we forget the natural things around us. Anything we're aware of can so easily be taken for granted or remain unnoticed.

Why is that?

Well, just look at the way we live these days! This is the age of technology and the more it speeds up, the faster we have to go to keep pace with it. Some of us are stretching ourselves to the limit to keep up with our machines! Press a button and you can send information to the other side of the world nearly instantaneously. We can sell and buy in cyberspace without ever coming face-to-face with a human being in the process. Mobile phones allow unlimited access at any time and any place to friends, family, and trade and business contacts. Many of us are working much longer hours than people were 25 years ago. We're bombarded on all sides by the media which feeds us a mind-boggling amount of information—good, bad and indifferent—24 hours a day. Whilst the plus side of this is we can now be much better informed than we were before and far more advanced in many respects, as a civilisation we are suffering from more stress-related problems and diseases than we were in previous generations.

Now, I'm not advocating that we all live reclusive lives in the country or emigrate to some remote area where people are living at a snail's pace. I'm not saying we have to give up the luxuries afforded by technology. Nor am I suggesting that we throw away our mobiles or stop reading newspapers! I'm just saying that this global village we all live in can get very noisy and crowded. It's small wonder that many of us have lost touch with Nature or the concept that we ourselves are part of it.

Actually, wherever you live, Nature is never very far away. Even amidst the concrete, glass and high-rise blocks of modern cities, you can still see it, touch it, and feel a sense of wonder about it. I remember once walking across Leicester Square in the heart of London's busy West End one summer evening and seeing the evening sky turn black with flocks of starlings coming together and preparing to settle for the night. It was gob-smackingly amazing. People were stopped in their tracks, staring up at the sky, hardly believing their eyes.

Nature is always there, just like the sun is always there behind the clouds. You'll find it in parks and village greens, in those small patches of grass in the middle of squares, in gardens and in window boxes, in the birds and the wildlife which live in our cities and towns. All we've got to do is become more aware of it. Then it's really not difficult to regain our connection with the earth and become more aware of our natural rhythms, instead of letting ourselves be driven by the speed of the culture.

What really helps is learning to "press the pause button" as one of my teachers (William Bloom) would say. If we can trigger a more gentle, spacious flow within ourselves and take some time to find the stillness within on a regular basis, it can make a huge difference to how we cope in our daily lives.

So how can we do that?

Well, it's quite simple. We extend the sort of thing we did in Exercise 1 (page 4) and Exercise 2 (page 5) and go into what's known as a guided visualisation (or meditation). You just need to bring certain images to mind and use your imagination. Exercise 3 is a great way to connect with, and feel a part of Nature. And it doesn't necessitate you going outdoors at all!

Here are just a few pointers before I take you into this:

- You can benefit most from doing this every day
- First thing in the morning is usually the best time, but some people may find it easier to do it in the evening
- Experiment to see which time of day suits you best.

At first, you may not be able to stay in this exercise for longer than a few minutes, but the more you practise it, the more time you'll want to spend with it because it feels so nice. The longer you can stay the better.

It's called "The Connection".

Exercise 3: The Connection

Put the phone on answer. Turn off the TV, radio, stereo, and computer. Close any doors or windows if you are in a draught. Make yourself comfortable in a sitting position with your back straight (supported by cushions if necessary) and with your feet placed firmly on the floor. If you are OK to sit cross-legged then do so, but make sure you are comfortable. You could lie down to do this but it's best not to as people tend to fall asleep when they lie down!

Close your eyes and bring your attention into the base of your torso and imagine that there is a line (or lines) of invisible energy extending from that part of you deep down into the earth beneath you. (You can imagine this like a big tap root or the roots of some great tree if you like.) Let these roots extend as deeply into the earth as you want them to go. As you extend them down, allow yourself to feel the safety and support of the earth.

Stay with this for a few moments.

Now, still keeping hold of your connection to the earth, bring your attention to your arms and both sides of your body. Imagine invisible lines of energy extending from there and outwards which connect you to the surface of the earth and to all the creatures which dwell upon it. Imagine they stretch out to include the vegetation, flowers, plants and trees which grow out of it, as well as to the seas and oceans and all the creatures which dwell there, too. Allow your energy to stretch outwards, imagining you are able to embrace all these things.

Stay with this for a few moments also.

Now, still feeling your connection deep into the earth and all across its surface, bring your attention to the crown of your head. Imagine more lines of energy extending out of you from there. Allow these energy lines to reach out to the treetops, to the hills and mountains, to the birds which fly in the sky. Then let the lines extend upwards and outwards even further—let them stretch up to the clouds, the sun, the moon and the stars. Let them extend into the galaxies beyond our planet and out into the universe beyond.

Stay with all this for as long as is comfortable. Enjoy your connection to all these things. When you are ready, come back slowly and sit for a while holding onto the feelings you experienced.

Exercise 3 is an adaptation of "The Connection" meditation by William Bloom.

Don't be surprised if you find that your response to this exercise changes according to how you're feeling at the time of doing it. Sometimes, in the early days, you may feel as though not much is happening. But if you can commit yourself to practising it regularly over a period of time, you'll start to notice subtle changes in your experience of it. Getting a sense of your connection to everything can make a huge difference to how you feel about yourself.

When you do feel deeply connected, I promise you that the sense of belonging, the feeling of being held in some great benign bubble and being part of something greater is a truly joyful and healing sensation.

Chapter 2

Mind–Body Connections

I'd like to change direction now and invite you to do something completely different! I want to help you experience what happens when we *consciously* tune into something that *doesn't* have benign and happy vibrations.

It would be really good if you could try Exercise 4 right now before reading any further. It will only take a few moments, but please make sure you've tried Exercise 1 (page 4) or Exercise 2 (page 5) *before* you do this.

Exercise 4: The Power of Thought

Close your eyes and think about a situation which was very unpleasant. Maybe it was something like a really bad argument or something you were very worried about. Whatever it was, *make sure you choose a scenario which **hasn't** given you any enjoyment at all.*

Once you've decided what it is you are going to focus on, I want you to bring it back to mind and allow yourself to really feel what it was like. Remember all the sensations which went with this situation. Really tune into these things.

Start doing this right now.

Hold onto the memory long enough for you to summon up all the feelings and sensations associated with this unpleasant issue. Be very aware of how you feel both *emotionally **and** physically.*

Then come back.

Make a note of how you felt doing that, noticing the emotions that came up, your feelings, and any sensations you had in your body. Notice where those feelings and sensations were and what they felt like. Make a quick note of what happened.

When you've done that, we're going to de-fuse that unpleasant memory and clear whatever feelings and sensations came up for you.

When you've finished noting down what happened for you, just close your eyes and quite quickly take yourself back to Exercise 1 (page 4) where you chose the memory of a special place in Nature which made you feel *really* good. Let yourself return to that place and recall the sense of well-being it gave you. Let those feelings flood every cell in your body and every fibre of your being. Imagine that when you breathe in, you're breathing in that wonderful place. And pretend that as you breathe out, you're letting go of that unpleasant experience. Keep doing that until it feels more comfortable inside.

You probably noticed that recalling unpleasant feelings made you feel very different from how you were when you tuned into Nature. Was it uncomfortable? Did you tense up or notice a difference in your posture while you were doing it? Perhaps you felt some physical sensation in your throat or your chest or your belly? Well, that's what can happen when you tune into something negative.

You've just demonstrated for yourself how moods and physical feelings can be created depending on where we place our attention. If we spend a lot of time tuning into negative thoughts and feelings or being subjected to a lot of pressure or living in a stressful environment, these things are not only making us feel bad but also affecting us on a biological level as well. In other words, they are affecting us physically.

You see, when we're stressed, tense and negative, what the body is actually doing is releasing specific hormones which circulate through the entire body and through every single one of the vital organs. These hormones are called *adrenaline* and *cortisol*. (By the way, for those of you who don't know, a hormone is like a chemical "messenger", frequently associated with mood changes which can transport a signal from one cell to another.)

Now, these hormones are perfectly natural and in essence there's nothing harmful about them. They can be incredibly useful when we're in a situation where we need to take instant action or to run away. They're part of what's known as our flight-or-fight response. In other words, they surge through our bodies and cause a state of heightened awareness, usually in times of danger. Thousands of years ago, early man would find himself activating these hormones when he was confronted by a sabre-toothed tiger. The modern equivalent might be swerving in our cars and slamming on the brakes to avoid knocking down a pedestrian!

Getting caught up in the frenetic pace of the culture or constantly living in a state of stress and anxiety can also make us produce these hormones. And here's where problems can arise. If this pressure becomes a daily occurrence for too long, we run the risk of becoming stressed out and off balance. The body simply can't cope well with being stimulated to that degree continuously, and if it is, it's going to suffer in one way, shape, or form. Depression may set in. Anger, frustration or aggression may erupt with little or no provocation. The immune system may become depleted, which lays you wide open for going down with a lot of colds or viruses. Energy levels can become very low. Sleep may be affected. Skin problems or digestive problems may develop, and generally life isn't a lot of fun.

On the other hand, happy, pleasurable experiences trigger a completely different set of hormones called *endorphins*. These hormones secrete a totally natural form of morphine and create feelings of well-being and euphoria when we're doing things we enjoy. They're also capable of deadening pain, boosting the immune system and are sometimes known as the "feel-good" hormones.

All pleasurable activities produce endorphins. So whenever you're doing something you love or having fun, you're flooding your body with all those healing molecules. We trigger endorphins when we experience the healing space of Nature. And we can do the same every time we practise "The Connection". There are an endless number of ways we can cause our bodies to release endorphins. Laughing will do it. So will making love. Spending time with a good friend or a beloved pet can do it, not to mention feeling warmth and kindness from another person or being in a safe and supportive environment.

Now, in case you're wondering how we know that these hormones can actually create the reactions I've described, it's been proved by some relatively recent scientific research which I want to tell you about.

Don't worry! I'm not going to get into any complicated scientific explanations, so don't turn the pages and skip to the next chapter. Just stick with me for a moment because I'm going to give you some very interesting background information on all this.

Endorphins were first discovered around the mid 1970s. At that time, scientists were looking to produce painkilling drugs which were less addictive and harmful than those currently on the market. This involved searching for what's known as the Opiate Receptor, which is a natural mechanism in the body, able to accept—rather than reject—a drug with an opium-type base. Scientists had been trying to find this receptor for quite a while and it was finally discovered by a neuro-scientist called Candace Pert.

In the process of all the research, what scientists found was that three vital body systems were all interlinked—the *nervous system* (the part of you which deals with information and sensation), the *immune system* (the part of you which fights infection and disease), and the *endocrine system* (the part which releases hormones and regulates a number of functions within the body and also plays a part in determining mood).

All these systems interact with the brain and run through every major organ. So what this research actually proved was that *the body is a flowing information system and that **every part of it** is engaged in that process.*

This discovery caused a big scientific breakthrough and gave birth to a whole new field of science with an incredibly long name—Psychoneuroimmunology or PNI for short. Everyone got very excited about it and it's cutting edge stuff in the scientific world right now.

However, the people who were probably even more excited about this news than the scientists were those favouring a holistic and alternative view of the human body. Why? Because it confirmed what the ancient sages of the East had been saying for thousands of years—*the body and mind are interconnected*. Basically what this means is that we don't just have a mind and a body. We have a body–mind, two halves of one complete whole!

This is why we can make chemical changes to our bodies by simply doing something we enjoy. As Candace Pert says in her book, *Molecules of Emotion*, which is about why we feel the way we feel: "Emotions and bodily sensations are...intricately entwined in a...network in which each can alter the other."

In other words: we can use our bodies to heal the mind. And we can also use our minds to heal our bodies. How amazing is that?

Our bodies are very important parts of our being. For a start, they carry us around and provide us with an environment in which to live. Unfortunately, we tend to take them for granted. Often we don't really bother about what's happening to them unless something goes wrong.

Many of us have virtually no awareness of our bodies because we are living in our heads most of the time! Some of us actually dislike our bodies to such an extent that we are constantly criticising our various shapes and forms. Not liking our bodies or being unkind to them is like being a relentlessly disapproving parent. And what do you think all that endless judgement and criticism is doing to us? Yup! It's triggering the stress hormones of adrenaline and cortisol and we know they're not good for us over extended periods. Our bodies are a part of Nature and have an animal quality. Just like domestic animals, they thrive on love, attention and nourishment. Think about what's happening to your body if it's criticised, ignored, taken for granted, or abused. You're going to make your body feel isolated, rejected and abandoned. And what is that going to do? More than likely, it will cause low self esteem and lack of confidence.

If we're faced with having to hack our way through the jungle, we need to be able to find ways of keeping ourselves in a reasonable state of balance both emotionally and physically. There's a nice, easy guided meditation I'd like to teach you which can help you to appreciate your body and start being kinder to yourself (Exercise 5). Doing this exercise will send healing endorphins to all your major organs and other vital systems in the body. Practise it on a daily basis and your body will start to feel loved and appreciated on a deep level. It's called "The Inner Smile".

Exercise 5: The Inner Smile

Sit comfortably with your back straight and propped up by cushions if necessary. You can sit cross-legged if this is comfortable, otherwise make sure your feet are placed firmly on the floor and your hands are either folded in your lap or resting on your knees.

Close your eyes. Breathe gently for a few breaths and become aware of your body as you sit on the chair, the sofa, or the floor.

Now bring to mind someone you know—or someone you've come across—who has soft, kind twinkling eyes. I'm sure you've all met someone like that. And just imagine that you, too, have kind, twinkly eyes, the kind of eyes that always have a bit of a sparkle and have a happy, laughing quality to them. Let your eyes become very kind and soft in this exercise. The eyes are actually exposed parts of the nervous system, and when you are putting a compassionate twinkle into your eyes, you are automatically sending a healing message directly into your nervous system.

So, with this kind, compassionate, twinkly smile, allow a physical smile to play around your lips and imagine you are smiling kindly up into your brain. Visualise all the folds and creases in its two hemispheres. Stay there for a moment and then silently thank your brain for all the work it does.

Still smiling kindly, bring your attention down to your heart and smile and twinkle appreciatively into that as you watch it pumping all the blood around your system. Again, stay for a few moments and then give it thanks.

Now, take your twinkling eyes down into your lungs which are gently moving in and out with your breath and smile kindly into all the little tubes within them. Stay for a few moments and give your lungs thanks for allowing you life-giving breath.

Then take your gentle smile to the front of your body on the right side, just under your right breast, This is where you will find your liver busily processing all those enzymes, and smile kindly and compassionately down at it. Give it thanks.

Travel with your eyes to the left side of your body where, tucked in behind the ribs and under the left breast, you'll find your stomach. Smile and twinkle kindly at that, too, as it works at digesting all the food you eat and give it thanks.

Now allow your kind, compassionate eyes to move towards your back, just above your waist, where you will find your kidneys which are so efficient at helping to remove the wastes from your body. Allow your eyes to rest there for a moment or two and give thanks to your kidneys. Then let your eyes travel to the front of your body in the area of your waist where you will find the large intestine looped up your right side, across and under the diaphragm and then downwards again on the left side of your body. Let your kind, twinkly smile rest upon this and the small intestine which is folded like a concertina in between the three sides of the large intestine. Smile benevolently down into these organs. Give them thanks for all the work they do in processing the food you eat.

Finally, allow your eyes to travel further down your body and smile kindly and compassionately at your genitals. Give them thanks too for the functions they perform and the pleasure they can give you.

As we come to the close of this exercise, imagine a happy smile like a crescent moon lying on its back stretched across your forehead. Imagine the same crescent moon smile stretched across your heart. Imagine that crescent moon smile stretched happily across your belly.

Rest for a few moments in this smile and then slowly and gently open your eyes.

Exercise 5 is a version of the "Inner Smile Meditation" by William Bloom.

Some people feel quite resistant to trying this exercise and it's often because they have issues about their body image and don't want to spend time focussing on any part of it. If this is true for you, remember the object of this guided meditation isn't anything to do with how we manifest on an outer level—whether we're tall, short, fat or thin, how we look facially, or whether we've got large feet or a big bum—we're looking inside at the organs which sustain our life and govern our health! For the most part, we take them almost completely for granted and if one organ (or more) isn't functioning optimally, we tend to not feel very kindly towards it.

Therefore, bearing in mind what I've been telling you about endorphins, it should now be clear that any thoughts of this ilk are very unhelpful. Your organs need love and appreciation to help them grow stronger. Even if you've got a healthy body, they still need kindness and gratitude to help you maintain your health and well-being.

This exercise can really help you do yourself a lot of good by directing endorphins into each different organ of your body.

If you have an existing meditation practise, try doing "The Inner Smile" followed by "The Connection" before you begin your own method. The combination of the two will then take you very easily and deeply into your usual mode of meditation and will give you a fantastic dose of endorphins for starting the day!

Chapter 3
Body Basics

Before we go any further I'd like have a brief look at basic body maintenance. This may sound strange, but, after all, our bodies are like the
vehicle in which we travel through life. Because our journeys often take us
over difficult terrain, from a very practical point of view we need to have a
means of transport which is road-worthy, to say the least!

Just as you'd put petrol in the tank of a car to keep it running, so your
body needs enough sleep, healthy food and water to keep you going. Think
of your vital organs as various parts of the engine. They all need to be kept
in good working order to ensure you don't grind to a halt on the motorway!
On top of that, all the other parts of you need to be functioning properly as
well to keep you on the road. We need to be aware of any part of us which
doesn't feel right and be prepared to get it checked out.

After all, if something goes wrong with your car, you take it to the garage,
don't you? We need to take care of our bodies just as well as we take care of
our cars.

Just think for a moment about what an amazing piece of machinery you
are! The body is constantly renewing itself. You get a new stomach lining
every five days. Millions of blood cells are always dying and being replaced by
new ones. Your fat cells fill and empty themselves repeatedly with the result
that they're changed every three weeks. Likewise, your skin keeps flaking off
imperceptibly and renewing itself about every three weeks as well. And in
addition, every year 98% of the atoms in your body are replaced!

But even though the body is capable of renewing itself, constant care
and attention is always needed because it can still go wrong or get ill. We're
all prone to the possibility of suffering damage physically, emotionally and
mentally. Some of us are blessed with good health, some get ill under pressure, some people are just tougher and fitter generally, and some are less
able to cope when the going gets tough. The ancient Chinese and Indian
cultures had medical systems which taught that healthy people who looked
after their bodies developed more inner resources and open-mindedness,
were more consciously connected to Nature, and were generally better able
to look after themselves and cope with the ups and downs of life. Their
medicine was focussed much more on prevention than on treatment and

repair. The Chinese systems of Tai Chi and Qi Gong as well as the Indian yoga postures and breathing exercises all grew out of these beliefs. Taking care of the body was a natural part of their everyday living and spiritual practise.

I'm therefore going spend a bit of time in this chapter running through some "Body Basics". These fall into three sections: diet, exercise, and sleep. I'm not going into these subjects in any great detail because each section merits a book in its own right, and there's plenty of information available written by people much better qualified than me in each of these areas (see the References and Suggested Reading section at the back of this book). However, I think it's really important to mention these things at an early stage so you can appreciate—if you don't already—how mindful we need to be about caring for our bodies.

Diet

Now, I'm not a nutritionist so I'm in no position to tell you how or what to eat. However, one thing I do know is that we definitely need to eat as healthily as possible, because if we don't, we're going to end up with energy problems and may find we have to deal with a whole pile of physical things going wrong as well.

When I say "eat healthily", I'm talking standard information which we've all heard about in the media, such as eating five portions of fruit and vegetables a day, steering away from cakes, pastries, sweets and biscuits, avoiding large amounts of convenience foods, and drinking around two litres of water each day. Many people already follow these guidelines, but if you aren't one of them, it makes sense to think about trying to improve your diet.

Why? Quite simply, eating the wrong foods can cause us a lot of problems from obesity to diabetes and from digestive disorders to heart disease. Also, research has shown that our emotional state and our moods are closely linked to the food we eat. So think about it. Do we really need to run the risk of giving ourselves any of these problems along with all the other challenges we encounter along the way?

Changing to a healthier diet doesn't mean you have to impose uncomfortable restrictions on yourself. You can start changing habits gently. Introducing just ONE new and healthier eating idea will give you a gradual appreciation of feeling better, which in itself can be a spur to doing more. You don't have to look anxiously and resentfully into the future and tell yourself you can never have another chocolate for the rest of your life! You could try making changes "just for today". For example: just for today, I won't have any chocolate/biscuits/alcohol, etc. Give yourself some appreciation and acknowledgement for achieving this when you've done it. Feel smug! Go on—it's OK! And then tomorrow, do the same thing all over again. That way you'll gradually build up momentum and start to see the beneficial changes you can bring about in yourself.

Diet and Eating Tips

Here are a few pointers to helping you on your way:

- Try keeping a diary of everything you eat for a week. Then do an honest assessment of your eating habits and make a note of things you might benefit from changing.

- If you know or suspect you may have an allergy to certain foods, try leaving them out of your diet for about three weeks and see if there's any improvement.

- Treat yourself to a health magazine and start reading up about developing a healthier diet and learning how to do it.

- If you're aware that you're drinking too much alcohol, smoking too many cigarettes, or comfort eating, try cutting down and see how you feel. If you find this doesn't work, then be prepared to seek help and advice from your GP, a nutritionist or a qualified practitioner in the appropriate field. (Always aim to choose one who has been recommended by someone you know, if possible.)

- You might like to consider going on a detox diet to cleanse your system. You'll also find this will help you to lose a bit of unwanted weight (see the Further Information and Suggested Reading at the back of the book if you want to go on this route).

- Drink more water! It helps us to digest our food and certainly helps with the elimination of it. It'll also help with cracked lips, dry skin, and stiff joints and is a good anti-ageing device!

- Read up about the benefits of doing a liver and gall bladder flush to improve physical and emotional health and well-being. It will get rid of gall stones, which clog up our systems, and help you to eliminate them painlessly in the comfort of your own home (see the Further Information and Suggested Reading section for more information on this).

- Switch to organic foods if you can afford it because, on average, they contain fewer pesticide residues and more vitamin C and other essential minerals. Non-organic meat contains a lot of steroids, hormones and antibiotics which have been fed to the animal to get it ready for market. Our bodies are better off without them.

- Don't wolf down your food. It's very stressful to your digestive system. Give yourself *time* to eat. Try adding an extra five minutes onto the time it usually takes you to eat a meal.

- Try not to eat on the hoof. In other words, don't eat your lunchtime sarnie while you're walking down the road!

Exercise

Another thing—if you're not already doing it—is to make sure you are getting enough exercise. Again this is something that can be introduced gradually. In fact going hell-for-leather into any aerobic regime when you're out of condition could set you up for further problems—so gently does it! If you're planning to start an exercise programme after a long period of inactivity, it's always best to check with your medical practitioner about whether it's suitable for you, especially if you suffer from any chronic condition or disability.

Getting more exercise needn't involve the expense of joining a gym. If you can afford it and it appeals to you, then by all means go that route. However, if it's going to be too much of a strain on your bank account, then you could investigate public sports and leisure centres in your area.

You don't even have to lash out and join any organisation if you prefer not to. Jogging, cycling and rebounding on a mini-trampoline are all activities you can do on your own. Some people may have preferences for particular forms of exercise like swimming, playing tennis or football. Or you may prefer work-outs that encourage you to flex and stretch your body, like yoga or Pilates. Use the internet to get information on where you might find some of these activities in your locality.

However, exercise doesn't necessarily involve engaging in sports or going to classes. You could just do a lot more walking whenever you can. Being more active needn't be a struggle or a bore. Try going for regular walks with a friend so you can talk while you walk! If you like dogs and don't have your own, you could offer to take a neighbour's dog for a walk on a regular basis. Be creative and find ways of making exercise as much fun as possible. That way you're more likely to stick to doing it.

Exercise Tips

Here are some more ideas to help you get started:

- Choose an exercise which you *like*! Otherwise you'll be rebelling against the whole idea from the word go!

- Walking is a very good weight-bearing activity to do because it helps your bones to stay healthy. You can pace yourself so you walk only as far as you can manage to begin with, and then try to extend this a little bit farther each day. Aim to spend about 30 minutes a day doing some brisk walking.

- If you take a bus to work, try walking to the next bus stop to catch your bus instead of getting on at the nearest place.
- Get together with some friends and start playing five-a-side football in the park on Sunday mornings
- Swimming is always very helpful—if you enjoy it—and can be fun, as well as a good way of losing a few pounds if done on a regular basis. If you have any heart problems it's the best form of exercise because it doesn't put any strain on your heart.
- If you have a physical problem or disability which makes ordinary exercise difficult or impossible, contact your GP's surgery for lists of places that provide for specialist needs and go along to some classes. Or try searching the internet for local classes in your area where you can move your body whilst sitting or lying down.
- Gardening is another activity which gives you plenty of exercise and fresh air. It gets you out into natural surroundings as well, which makes a nice combination for those to whom it has some appeal.
- If you enjoy dancing—then *dance*! There's no better exercise. It's free form and fun and releases lots of endorphins!

Sleep

We also need to be mindful of whether we're getting enough sleep, which is a big factor in dealing with stress. Sleep is a very important time for healing and rejuvenation. Research has shown that sleep deprivation can cause ill health and make us prone to heart disease, obesity, high blood pressure, stroke and depression.

Who wants those?

Sleeping Tips

Here are some tips to help with sleeping better:

- Try not to eat a heavy meal late in the evening. You'll be making your digestive system start working just when it thinks it's time to have a rest!
- Avoid stimulants like drinking tea, coffee and alcohol late at night.
- Try a winding down process to get you into relaxation/sleeping mode. A warm candlelit bath with nice soothing music in the background before going to bed is a great way of doing this. You could

add a few drops of lavender oil to the bathwater which would help you to relax.

- It's best not to watch television in bed as it can be too stimulating for the mind before sleeping. Do that in another room and keep your bed just for sleeping and making love.

- If you spend a lot of time on the computer, make a point of finishing whatever you're doing and turning it off at least an hour before going to bed. Otherwise you'll find that it can have the effect of keeping your mind too active just when it needs to calm down and get ready for sleep.

- If you don't have regular hours for going to sleep and waking, try to introduce a routine where you go to bed and wake up at roughly the same time each day.

- Use Exercise 2 (page 5) where you go to a safe place in your mind. This will fill you with endorphins and send you into a good healthy slumber.

- Having a more active lifestyle or taking regular exercise is an excellent way of ensuring a good night's sleep. So is getting plenty of fresh air on a regular basis.

- Try drinking a cup of chamomile tea before going to bed. It's excellent for inducing sleep.

And finally, I just want to talk about something that will really make your engine purr!! *Enjoyment* and *pleasure*!

Yes, doing enjoyable, pleasurable things is really good for us (because it releases a lot of endorphins) and is an essential part of body maintenance! We need to do as much of it as we can because it's a very nurturing and healing thing to do and a really good way of combating stress.

You now know that when the body–mind goes into stress it's causing a chemical reaction which isn't good for your health. Therefore, we need to find whatever antidotes we can to counteract this damage.

We've seen how we can change our moods from negative to positive and experience a sense of well-being by using simple visualisation techniques. So, wouldn't it be nice if we could start looking at how to do this more frequently by using other methods? That way we could learn to help ourselves reach a better state of balance on a mental, emotional and physical level of our being on a day-to-day basis.

It's not so difficult. Exercise 6 will give you something else to try:

Exercise 6: Working with the Best Things in Your Life

Take a moment right now to write down all the things in life which give you pleasure. Make a list of all the wonderful things in your life, all the things which give you tremendous enjoyment and which you absolutely adore.

But, *please* don't include anything which requires you taking some substance to feel that enjoyment, like alcohol, nicotine or drugs. Just choose things you can naturally enjoy without any outside inducement.

Divide this list up under the following headings:

- People and animals
- Places
- Activities
- Smells, colours and textures
- Spiritual symbols or idols (Jesus, Buddha, Star of David etc.,—but don't worry if you don't have anything in this section)

Now put an check mark beside all those things which are easily accessible and readily there for you in everyday life (for example, anything that doesn't require travelling or going to lengthy arrangements to experience).

Make yourself a promise that you will engage with or in at least *one* of those checked things at least *once* a week, and more frequently, if possible.

Exercise 6 is an endorphin exercise by William Bloom.

Before we finish this chapter, make yourself another promise: that you will, at all times, be aware during your daily activities of anything you encounter—which may or may not be on the above lists—which gives you pleasure or enjoyment. Then, when you notice yourself enjoying whatever it is, you will *consciously* focus on it and allow yourself to really feel how much you enjoy it! Notice the changes in your posture and breathing, the relaxation of the muscles in your face and your body, the way your spirits lift.

Just absorb all those nice feelings as though you were a piece of blotting paper and imagine you're soaking them up!

Enjoy!

Chapter 4

Moods, Feelings and Emotions

B esides looking after the body, we also need to find out how best to look after our moods and emotions. As William Bloom says, "Our emotional life needs the same care, attention and friendship as our bodies." Why? Because your body responds to the way that you *feel*—your feelings are all about your emotions and your emotions affect your mood.

We've already seen how damaging it can be if we focus on negative emotions. Think back to Exercise 3 (page 7) where you recalled a situation which was very unpleasant. Remember how your body felt when you thought about those uncomfortable events? You felt the "acid" of adrenalin and cortisol, rather than the "honey" of endorphins.

Moods like happiness, contentedness and peacefulness will trigger endorphins, but moods which are angry, sad and fearful will trigger adrenalin and cortisol instead. Which would you rather have coursing around your body?

Managing moods and emotions doesn't mean you don't go through all the usual ups and downs of life anymore. You can't prevent that, I'm afraid! It just means that you're able to handle your feelings in more appropriate ways and make life a bit easier for yourself. There are a number of techniques you can use, such as the Emotional Freedom Technique (EFT) and EmoTrance (more about these later), that enable you to help yourself target problems and dissolve distress on many levels. This kind of emotional "self-management" means you have ways to shake off many problems, rather like gathering up remedies and sticking plasters to keep in a First Aid Kit! The more solutions and antidotes you have to make life less of a bumpy ride, the better you are at bouncing back from any difficulties you may encounter along the way.

Emotional management is about being aware of what may lurk beneath that feeling of hurt or anger. It's about learning ways to handle sadness and pain, about taking responsibility for our actions and decisions, or keeping to commitments we've made. It's also about managing relationships better and knowing when you project your own reactions and judgements onto other people. It's to do with being assertive rather than angry and aggressive. It's also about learning to compromise rather than always trying to get our own way.

In the first part of this chapter, I'm going to focus on looking for telltale signs which can signal our emotions need some care and attention. Strange though it may seem, we may think we're always aware of what's going on inside of us, but often we're kidding ourselves. We bury stuff. We hide it. We deny it. We forget it was there in the first place until it jumps out and trips us up!

One way of becoming aware of what's going on inside is by noticing any physical symptoms, such as a change in appetite, extreme tiredness, upset stomach or alternate constipation/diarrhoea, weight gain or loss, high blood pressure, general aches and pains, headaches, or sexual problems, etc.

Life factors can also disrupt your emotional health and leave you feeling sad or anxious. For example, losing your job or not getting enough work if you're self employed, death of a loved one, a close friend, a family member or a beloved pet, getting divorced, moving home or relocating to another part of the country, suffering illness or injury, money problems, and so on.

You can even experience emotional wobbles when good things are happening in your life, such as getting married. All that planning for the wedding can be really stressful. Being promoted is another instance. You might get very worried thinking about the added responsibility and feel anxious about whether you'll come up to scratch. Having a baby brings challenges within all the joy. Huge changes are taking place throughout the body and mind of the pregnant mum. In addition, there is often major anxiety going on for the dads-to-be who might be getting stressed out thinking about the responsibility and changes in life style which may have to be made.

Everyone has emotions and there's absolutely nothing whatsoever wrong with them. They're perfectly natural human feelings. It's when we start denying them, trying to control them too rigidly, or getting swamped by them that we make life more difficult for ourselves and other people.

Most of us are already trying to manage our daily ups and downs to one degree or another and a lot of our free time is spent on trying to balance our emotions as well as relax. We do this through reading or indulging in some retail therapy, watching films or TV, or spending time with friends and loved ones. But it's not a particularly conscious (or even successful) way of doing it.

In Part II of this book, I'm going to explain how to use specific therapeutic techniques to help you through difficult emotional issues. For the moment, however, I want to explain about mood enhancers and some very basic emotional monitoring and self-care. Becoming more aware of any changes which we experience in mood and body means we're then in a position to administer whatever "first aid" is required. Exercise 1 (page 4) and Exercise 2 (page 5) and those pleasure-giving ingredients of your life in Exercise 5 (page 13), are not only useful for changing moods, they can also be helpful in managing emotions.

Exercise 7 incorporates some of the endorphin work we've already done and adds in another dimension to it. It's a great thing to do if your mood is low or if you're tired or generally needing some TLC.

Exercise 7: Collapse and Retreat Endorphin-Style

Next time you're feeling low, allow yourself to collapse onto your bed or the sofa and cover yourself up with a duvet or warm throw. It sometimes helps to let yourself assume a foetal position or curl up physically like a small animal in a burrow. You can put the duvet right over your head if you want! Take comfort from being in this little sanctuary, knowing that you are safe and that everyone else is going to back off and leave you in peace.

Enjoy snuggling down into your chosen position. Feel the weight of your body on the mattress or the sofa. Imagine you can feel the forces of gravity pulling on you and let your body collapse inwards and downwards.

Now, start thinking about some of those things which you listed in Exercise 6 (page 21). Bring to mind some of the things you particularly *love*. Be aware of how conjuring images of these things in your mind gives you a sense of pleasure. Turn up the volume a bit on that sense of feeling good and breathe it in deeply into the very core of you.

Switch on your "Inner Smile" and smile down into your body. Sweep your body with the smile. You can do this quite quickly, like scanning with a searchlight. Then, return to thinking about those things you enjoy so much. Notice how your body responds when you think about them. Notice how this creates a feeling of those sensations coursing through you like a river. Start guiding this flow of feel-good sensations through all of your body, directing them into every part of you. "Simply by thinking about a particular part of your body, you create what is called a *neural pathway*, a connection between your mind–brain and that body part. Using your creative mental faculties, you can deliberately imagine and guide good feelings through your body."*

Have fun sending this river of endorphins wherever you want it to go in your body. You might find yourself dozing off in the middle of it, but that's fine. When you awake, yawn, stretch, wiggle your toes and make conscious contact with your body again. Then very slowly get up.

This exercise is a very good one for improving your mood!

Exercise 7 is an endorphin exercise by William Bloom.
* From *The Endorphin Effect* by William Bloom

Another good way of raising your emotional state is to sing. Yes! Singing is incredibly uplifting. Why do you think religions all over the world have used singing and chanting as an integral part of their worship? We have to breathe more efficiently when singing in order to allow more oxygen down into the lungs and this can have the effect of calming the mind and opening the heart. A well-oxygenated body produces healthier, happier and more alert states of mind. Singing has also been found to boost the immune system, lower heart rate, decrease blood pressure, reduce stress and depression, and enhance feelings of relaxation, mood and confidence. There's also evidence that it helps Alzheimer's patients re-find their ability to socially engage with others, and that it improves breathing capacity in asthma sufferers. In addition, singing triggers a rush of endorphins—which of course makes you feel good!

Don't worry if you think you haven't got much of a voice. It doesn't matter. This isn't about becoming a professional singer! This is for fun!

Here's some things you could try to get yourself singing:

- Make the most of your bathroom acoustics (they usually provide something of a built-in echo chamber) and start singing in the bath!

- Sing along with a CD by one of your favourite singers or bands. You can do this either at home or in the car. Or try some Karaoke!

- Join a choir. It's fun singing with others. Your local church would be a good place to start, but there may be other possibilities in your locality.

- Watch out for any workshops in the UK run by Chris James, an internationally renowned teacher of Voice and Sound. Chris has the amazing ability to make a roomful of shy, retiring people feel OK about standing up and singing their hearts out! I once sat in on a platform workshop of his at a Mind Body Spirit Exhibition some years ago, where he had just half an hour to demonstrate what he could do. By the end of that time, 50-odd people were on their feet, singing and clapping their hands and providing en masse backing vocals for him! It was fantastic, and great fun! Everyone had a smile on their face and he made it all feel so easy (see the Further Information and Suggested Reading section at the back of the book for more information).

- Investigate *overtone singing*. This is an ancient form of harmonic singing and chanting which has been used in sacred ceremonies for hundreds of years. What happens is that you learn how to manipulate certain harmonics and overtones in the voice in a way that can produce two notes at the same time. The effects of mastering this technique are extraordinarily spectacular, and you can produce amazingly beautiful sounds from within yourself which are very healing and uplifting. Jill Purce is an expert in this field and details of her cassettes, CDs, workshops and lectures can be found in the Further Information and Suggested Reading section at the back of this book. ·

You can also help your mood by taking care not to catch other people's mind states. Some folks can bring us down very easily if we're not careful. Have you ever noticed how sometimes you're badly affected by people who are full of whinges and complaints? Some people grumble and carp all day long, day after day—and anything goes! They'll complain about the weather, about the government, about what's on the news or in the papers, about work, about their children, about the queue in the supermarket, about public transport, or about how much they have to do. The possibilities are endless!! Listen to it for long enough and it starts to have an effect on you. It brings you down. It gets you into complaining as well!

If you find yourself in the company of someone who does this regularly, either make a strenuous attempt to bring some positivity into the conversation, or keep the time spent with them to a minimum. Better still, avoid them completely if you're feeling rather vulnerable yourself! Please note, I'm not suggesting that you should "shut out" someone who's genuinely going through a bad patch and needs to unload. I'm talking about people who just have a habit of being negative about everything on a daily basis.

Another very simple and effective way of regularly keeping track of how we're feeling is to start keeping a journal (Exercise 8). Now, before you start thinking that you have to write lengthy descriptions each and every day addressed to "Dear Diary", let me tell you, journaling doesn't have to be like that!

I also want to make it clear that you don't have to be a good writer to keep a diary, nor is it important to be good at spelling or grammar. All you have to do is to write down how you feel about life, events, people, your job, your significant other (or lack of one!) or whatever. Journaling is simply writing about how you're feeling.

Exercise 8: Keeping a Journal

Buy yourself a nice fat notebook and make some time to sit down regularly and write! A good time to start is on a Sunday morning when the house is quiet.

You don't have to write every day. Do it when something is "up" in your mind and you need to "talk about it". You can write about anything and everything. Don't stop to think, edit or criticise what you're putting down as you write. You're simply expressing your thoughts and feelings and it's a wonderfully releasing process.

If you need to pour out your heart, *then do so!*

If you're feeling fantastic, aligned and in flow, then *write about that!*

If your mind is full of something that happened last night with so-and-so and you can't get it out of your mind. *Marvellous!*

Got the idea? Start writing in that notebook and see how much clearer you feel once you've done it!

I recommend that you keep doing this for around 6 to 8 weeks. This will give you a chance to see how you can benefit. Read through what you've written after about a month. Notice the patterns of difficulty which emerge and in what areas of your life they predominate. This will show you areas where you need to work on yourself with other techniques.

Negative stuff may come up. If so, *let it*! People who've schooled themselves into working with affirmations might throw up their hands in horror at the thought of writing about whinges and perceived failings. But actually, as they say, it's much better out than in! Lots of people are surprised at how much negative self-talk they engage in, and *it's really important to be aware of it!*

Keeping a journal is a great way to offload *safely.* There's no-one on the receiving end no-one is going to judge or misunderstand what you say. And you can say *anything* you like without any worries about starting World War III!

An additional and very useful journaling process for getting stuff off your mind is a technique called "The Morning Pages". You'll find this technique in a workbook by Julia Cameron called *The Artist's Way*. This technique involves writing non-stop at the beginning of each day in a stream-of-consciousness writing. This is a great method for finding out what's going on inside of you. I recommend that you read the book. It's not just for artists or those aspiring to be artists. It's helpful for anyone who's trying to find out what stops them from doing the things which they want to do in life.

Writing can be a wonderfully therapeutic process and there's an extremely helpful exercise you can do when you need to tell someone exactly what you feel and think about them, but just can't bring yourself to do so. I've given this exercise to countless clients and students over the years and those who've tried it confirm its effectiveness in helping them to let go of a troubling situation or finding a new attitude towards it.

Use Exercise 9 for any situation that's reached an impasse, where communication has broken down, where all negotiations have come to naught, where you feel totally helpless or victimised, where the other person seems incapable of understanding your point of view, or where you feel you've been particularly hurt, etc.

Exercise 9: Write Them A Letter

Organise yourself with some private space, something to write on (i.e., paper, notebook or computer) and make it clear to anyone else in the house that you don't want to be disturbed. You can have music playing in the background if you wish or do this exercise in silence. However, you must do this exercise in *one* go and complete it the same day you begin it.

Start writing this person a letter: Dear _____

Without censoring *anything*, write down *everything* you feel about this situation or person. Describe the pain/anger/sadness/grief or whatever as graphically as you can. Tell them what you think of them—no holds barred! You can call them names and use whatever swear words seem appropriate if you wish. **You are never going to send this letter and no copy of it will exist after you've finished writing it, so you can feel free to say whatever you want to say without holding back in any way.**

Don't worry about making the letter grammatically correct. Don't worry about spelling. Don't try to edit it as you write. *Just write it!*

Tears and anger may arise, sadness and grief also. Let it all out and onto the page. Speak out everything you've felt or been holding on to. Let it all go.

When you've finished, read it through and sign your name.

Then either burn it or tear it up into small pieces and flush it down the loo.

On no account should you keep this letter amongst your belongings and *never, never* send it

You can also use this letter-writing exercise to address someone who is dead and therefore leaves you in a position where you no longer have any opportunity to clear things with them.

As you progress through this book, you'll be learning about many other tools and techniques to help you with various different issues and events in your life. Learning to read the signs signalling a major wobble ahead, understanding your moods and handling them better, and starting to be generally more aware of how you are on a daily basis, are understandings which will serve you incredibly well on your journey to find your river.

I'm going to end this chapter with a three key things to remember about difficult times and wobbly emotions:

- When you're relaxed, you can't feel negative. That's right! It's a physical impossibility! So make relaxation a priority!

- Remember: *nothing lasts forever*! Write this out and pin it up somewhere to remind you when you're going through difficult times.

- Remember to keep your sense of humour!

Chapter 5
Relaxation and Pacing

With all the pressure and stresses of the culture we live in, it's really important to try to find time for regular relaxation. In this chapter I will tell you about some methods to relax which I've found to be particularly effective.

When I talk about relaxing, I don't mean collapsing into an exhausted heap at the end of a day. Nor do I mean resorting to the aid of alcohol or other substances to help you wind down. I'm talking about natural ways to relax and pace yourself so you can ride the challenges better, feel more balanced and still have some energy reserves.

Some people find it very hard to relax and feel compelled to keep driving themselves from one activity to the next. Believe me, we are not designed to go through life without regular periods of relaxation each day.

Just like everything in Nature, we have cycles which our bodies automatically follow even though we aren't necessarily aware of them. In the same way that Nature is subject to particular rhythms, like the monthly phases of the moon and the times when the animal kingdom follows feeding, breeding and resting cycles, we too have rhythms which ebb and flow within us. The *Circadian Rhythm* happens once a day and tells us when it's time to get up or go to sleep. The *Ultradian Rhythm* happens more than once a day and influences our energy and concentration levels. The *Infradian Rhythm*, which lasts longer than a day, affects things like menstrual cycles and our response to the changing seasons.

The Ultradian Rhythm is incredibly useful regarding relaxation because it gives us a unique and personal tempo to follow in terms of pacing and resting ourselves each day. Once we've learnt to tune into it, it can show us when we're naturally ready to be active and when we need to rest.

So what is this Ultradian Rhythm?

It's a natural rhythm that supports alertness and activity for a period of between 90 to 120 minutes followed by a resting period lasting around 10 to 20 minutes that repeats itself all through our waking day. During the active cycles, our mental and physical abilities are functioning well, but during the resting periods, we're less able to concentrate and may start feeling a bit dreamier or even sleepy. Often, when these energy dips come, we resort to having a cup of tea or coffee, or smoking a cigarette in order help us continue working.

The trick is *not* to do this! If we can listen to our bodies and follow this rhythm, we can become more efficient and productive during our active periods. This is Nature's own way of helping us to pace ourselves.

Ernest Rossi, who pioneered much of the research into this area, named the process of flowing with this rhythm "The Ultradian Healing Response". I call it simply: "Natural Pacing and Relaxation".

How do we work with it?

Basically, towards the end of the active cycle, the body gives us numerous cues which signify that it needs a break. These signals indicate depleted energy reserves and should be heeded because otherwise it can lead to what Rossi calls "The Ultradian Stress Syndrome". You'll know if you're heading for this state because you'll start getting more tired, lose focus, get irritable, make mistakes and be more prone to having accidents.

Does that sound familiar?

Ignoring these signals and shrugging off the need for a break means that the body starts getting flooded with stress hormones—and you know what they can do! Paradoxically, at this point, if you carry on pushing yourself instead of taking a rest, you'll get an energy surge or *second wind* that makes you feel like you don't need a break. Don't be fooled by this! What's actually happening is that you're experiencing an adrenaline *high*. This simply masks the tiredness, over-rides the lack of concentration and leaves you feeling completely wiped out later. If you make a habit of doing this, you'll end up in full Ultradian Stress Syndrome that causes you to become hyperactive, manic, irritable, angry, rude, unsympathetic and selfish. Other people will notice this happening much more quickly than you!! It's pure workaholic behaviour and I'm sure you've all met a few people who either get themselves easily into this state or appear to live in it most of the time!

So what do we have to do? It's very simple. Just watch out for the following:

- Yawning or sighing
- Needing to move or stretch your body
- Noticing tension and aches in your body along with a feeling of tiredness
- Hesitating, putting things off or not feeling able to continue working
- Needing to urinate
- Feeling hungry
- Your mind wanders, you forget words, you lose concentration

- Making mistakes and getting careless
- Feeling low or depressed and emotionally vulnerable
- Getting distracted by fantasies

As soon as you notice one or more of the above, you need to *stop* what you are doing and take 10 to 20 minutes time out (Exercise 10). Your body will then re-balance and re-boot. Afterward your energy perks up and you'll feel fresher, clearer and able to continue working.

A few tips before trying this method:

- Commit yourself to a seven-day trial of it before you decide if it's for you or not.

- Keep a daily note of when you get up and notice what times you're getting the cues to stop. This way, you begin to familiarise yourself with your personal rhythms.

- Once you've identified your Ultradians, it's easier to follow them without much effort and simply respond to your body's needs. You'll find that with practise you'll get better and better at taking these breaks so they fit in seamlessly with your lifestyle or job.

Exercise 10: Natural Pacing and Relaxation

Once you notice any of the signs I listed previously, stop whatever you're doing.

Go and sit down in a space where you can be quiet and alone. Bring your focus to the automatic process of breathing in and out. This is a good way of slowing down. Notice which part of your body feels most comfortable, allow yourself to sink into that area and let that feeling of comfort spread into the rest of your body.

You don't have to do anything else!

If you tend to be very mentally active (i.e., mostly tuned into left-brained linear, logical thought processes), at this stage, you're likely to become aware of your racing thoughts or anxieties about things to do. Don't worry! Just notice this happening and keep bringing your attention back into that comfort area and enjoying its soothing quality. The more you practise this, the better you'll become at detaching from what's going on mentally.

On the other hand, if you're more right-brained (i.e., an artistic-intuitive person), you might find yourself floating into a limbo-land where there aren't many thoughts or feelings.

Either way is fine. What's happening when you do this is that you're handing over control to the body instead of letting the mind rule. After a short while, you may find yourself becoming sleepy. If so, allow yourself to doze off a little if you want.

You'll naturally remain in this state for between 10 to 20 minutes. The length of time varies according to the individual, and you'll need to practise this exercise a number of times to get a feel of how long you need personally. The active cycle of your body's rhythms naturally kicks back in again after about 10 to 20 minutes, signalling that the resting period is finished for now. When this happens, open your eyes and maybe stretch a little or take a couple of deep breaths. Enjoy re-establishing contact with the room you are in and your normal waking state. Notice how rested and good you feel. Return to whatever you were doing before and be alert for the next set of signals your body will give.

Carry on following your rhythms for the rest of your working day. Get into the habit of doing this on a daily basis and you'll soon notice the difference!

Exercise 10 is derived from Ernest Rossi's book *The 20-Minute Break*.

You can use this technique to help you in many other ways such as regulating your diet and weight, improving your sex life, and increasing vitality and focus in senior citizens. If you'd like to find out more about working your Ultradian rhythms or about Ernest Rossi's other books, you'll find details in the Further Information and Suggested Reading sections at the back of this book.

I can hear you protesting already that you're much too busy to take time out several times a day to do this exercise! You may believe that if you didn't keep going nothing would ever get done or that because you have a family, there's never any time for rest and relaxation!

I totally understand that it's harder for some of us to take time out and relax. This may be because you are in the habit of never letting up or because your job doesn't give you the freedom to take breaks when you need them—or whatever. I also appreciate that at times there simply isn't the opportunity to have a break when you need it because you're going through one of those nightmare days when there's too much to do and not enough time to do it!

In these and other circumstances, you might like to try an alternative version of the above exercise that I call "Basic Pacing" (see Exercise 11). In this exercise you leave out the relaxation bit. Instead, you keep changing the tempo of your activities to coincide with the active–resting rhythms already described. It's not as beneficial for you as Exercise 10, but it will help you work at a pace that is more natural and therefore less stressful.

It's very important when you're using Exercise 11 to avoid certain activities when changing from sedentary or desk-bound work to something more active. "The key to turning these activities into meaningful ultradian healing breaks…is to avoid doing anything difficult, strongly goal-directed, or requiring concentration…(for example) strenuous exercise, self-improvement tasks, programme or rushed activities, highly directive mind work, operating machinery, time pressure tasks, decision making and new creative work."[*]

* From *The 20-Minute Break* by Ernest Rossi.

Exercise 11: Basic Pacing

Watch out for your energy dip signals as listed on page 32–33.

Get used to monitoring your rhythms and make a note of when they happen.

When you notice the cues for rest, *stop* what you're doing and *switch activities* for 10 to 20 minutes. (With practise, you'll know how long you need personally.)

Rule of Thumb:

- If you've been sedentary, *get up and move.*
- If you've been active—*sit down or slow down!*
- If you are working on a computer, you *must* get up and move away from it.

Sitting for hours on end in front of a screen:

- is bad for your eyes
- causes your mind to race
- gives you a higher exposure to electro-magnetic pollution

Working on a computer means you are simultaneously sedentary *and* mentally active during your 90 to 120 minute cycles of natural activity time! When you take a break from your computer, get up and move but make sure your alternative activities allow you to move your body *and* rest or de-focus your mind (e.g., take a gentle walk round the block, water the plants, do some photocopying, load the washing machine, or do some light housework, etc.).

Exercise 11 is derived from Ernest Rossi's book *The 20-Minute Break*.

One final point: if you feel guilty or anxious at the idea of doing either Exercise 10 (page 33) or Exercise 11, or if you consider you will be wasting your time by doing any form of relaxation, check out Chapters 12 and 13 in Part 2. There you will find details of how to use Emotional Freedom Technique and EmoTrance. Either of these techniques will help you to dissolve your anxiety or resistance to driving yourself so hard. Once you've dealt with this problem, you should feel able to let yourself relax every now and again.

Another way of getting some relaxation in a busy day is to learn to take a short rest period called a Power Nap (Exercise 12, page 36). This nap lasts no longer than 30 minutes and you can choose how long you make it according to how much time you can allow in any one day. You only take this break *once* and a good time to do it is just after lunch. Most people become tired in the afternoon even if they've had 8 hours sleep the night before. Research has shown that 20 to 30 minutes of additional sleep after lunch provides more rest than an extra half hour taken in the morning.

You may have found in the past that sleeping in the afternoon makes you wake up feeling even more tired. This is because you've allowed yourself to sleep for more than half an hour. What has happened is that you've sunk into a deeper level of sleep which makes waking harder and causes you to feel groggy afterwards. As long as you don't take more than 30 minutes for your Power Nap you'll remain in a light sleep and wake up feeling relaxed, refreshed and invigorated.

Exercise 12: The Power Nap

Find a place where you can do this without interruption for at least 10 minutes but no more than 30 minutes. You may wish at first to set an alarm to ensure you come out of it after a set period of time. If you do this, make sure it isn't an alarm that's shrill and going to give you a fright when you hear it! (Most mobile phones have got an alarm on them so you could use that.) If you want to plug yourself into some gentle soothing music while you're doing it—Classical, New Age, Meditation or Ambient Zero-Beat Music—to help with the relaxation process, then by all means do so, but keep the volume soft.

Sit in a comfortable chair with a head rest or lie down on the sofa or the bed or on some cushions on the floor. Close your eyes. Start noticing your breathing and spend a few moments observing the process of breathing in and out. Notice which part of your body feels most comfortable (it's often the lower abdomen), and imagine yourself sinking into that area. Imagine you're in an elevator which is taking you down from the top floor (your head) to your belly (the basement). Imagine the energies of your brain sinking down as if drawn by gravity. As this happens, your breathing should automatically start slowing down.

If thoughts come, just let them. That's what thoughts do. They tumble one upon another. Observe this and don't get hooked into any of them. Just watch for the next thought and allow it to pass though and out. Your mind is simply letting go of information. Don't worry—you'll be able to retrieve that information later if you think you need it.

If there's any tension in your neck and shoulders, imagine it dissolving and sinking down to your lower stomach. Check to see if there's any tension in your abdomen and do the same.

Keep a gentle awareness on your breath and in a short while, you may find yourself beginning to dream or fall into a conscious slumber. If you want, at this point you can bring to mind some of those comforting images of being out in Nature that you explored in Exercise 1 (page 4) and Exercise 2 (page 5).

Stay in this place of relaxation until either your alarm goes off or you awaken naturally after 10 to 30 minutes. Then open your eyes, take a few breaths and stretch gently. Within a minute or two you'll be wide awake again and feeling the benefits of this relaxation.

My final suggestion for relaxation is Exercise 13, which takes around 20 to 30 minutes. It's a technique I learnt a long time ago that I've always found to be very effective. It can be done at any time of the day but it's best to do it when you're not pushed for time. You can do it at night and go to sleep in it if you like. It's called The Blue Mist.

Exercise 13: The Blue Mist

Find a comfortable place to lie down that is warm and free from draughts. Your bed is probably the best place, but there's no harm in doing this on some cushions on the floor. If your sofa isn't long enough to stretch out on properly, don't use it because it's easy to end up lying in an awkward position. If it helps, put on some soft, gentle music, but don't have it too loud.

Cover yourself with a light throw and lie on your back with a cushion behind your head. Bring your attention into your breathing, noticing your in breath and your out breath. Keep focussing on your breathing for about ten breaths.

Imagine the most beautiful blue colour—the colour blue that appeals to you most of all. Imagine it's like a mist or like the dry ice that's often used on TV pop shows to give the effect of swirls of mist covering the floor of the stage and wafting around the feet of the singers.

Imagine this blue mist being the comfortable temperature of a warm breeze that is totally benign and utterly soothing. And as you think about it, imagine it entering your body through the soles of your feet.

Visualise it slowly drifting up through your legs and into your thighs and buttocks. Imagine it swirling up through your abdomen, into your chest and up to your shoulders. Imagine it drifting down into your arms and fingers. See it moving up through your neck and into your head. You are now totally filled with this beautiful blue mist.

Let your mind scan your body to check that the blue mist has filled every single nook and cranny. If you notice any gaps, send some more blue mist in there. Keep your awareness on the mist and imagine it slowly permeating every bone, muscle and fibre, every cell, every organ in your body. There is no part of you that isn't filled with this beautiful blue mist. Enjoy the idea of this healing mist circulating freely through your body. Imagine it's melting away all the tension, all the anxieties, all the aches and pains. This mist is healing and relaxing. Allow it to flow through you and if you find you're getting a bit sleepy, let yourself nod off.

If you don't get drowsy, then stay in the relaxed state generated by this exercise for about 20 to 30 minutes. Then come back, open your eyes, stretch and very slowly, get up.

If you find it hard to visualise, try to get a sense of the *feel* of this mist instead.

You may find that mixing and matching Exercises 10 through to 13 suits you better than sticking rigidly to one or the other. You might find that doing Natural Pacing and Relaxation mixed in with the Basic Pacing works better for you according to the pressures of the day. Or you might prefer to do Basic Pacing and one Power Nap each day. Or try Natural Pacing and Relaxation most days and Blue Mist at weekends.

It's up to you. Try all of them to see what works best for you.

By the way, I could not have written this book without doing the pacing and relaxing exercises for myself! Trying to fit in time to write during busy working days isn't easy and the temptation is always there to push yourself too hard in an effort to get more done. But it never works that way.

Tune into your natural rhythms and flow with them. Trust me! It'll make the world of difference!

Finding the River

Chapter 6

Meditation

Meditation and relaxation are often mentioned in the same breath but they are, in fact, subtly different. The main distinction between them is that whilst relaxation is concerned with letting go of tension in mind and body (often resulting in sleep), meditation is about achieving a state of being both relaxed *and* alert at the same time.

It may surprise you to learn that meditation is a perfectly natural practice. Do you ever recall experiencing the peace that comes from contemplating a beautiful view or sunset? Stroking a cat? Feeling the warm sun on your body as you listen to waves lapping on the shore? I'll bet you do. Well, that's a form of meditation. That's what happens when you sink into a deep focus on something. The babbling of the mind subsides and we ease into a more tranquil space within ourselves.

We've actually been meditating since we were first born. Have you ever offered a finger to a small baby to hold? Have you noticed how, when it grasps the finger in its tiny fist, it seems to be wrapped in the wonder of this new experience? You can see from the look on its face that nothing else matters at that moment. That's meditation! Meditation is all about giving one-pointed focus to something and letting all other extraneous thoughts go.

As we grow up, our ability to do this changes. Toddlers might get absorbed in things like a large leaf that's blown down from a tree or sailing a toy boat in the bath. As adults we may find we're brought to a halt by the sight of the gorgeous colours of autumn foliage, or stopped in our tracks by the sight of a squirrel crossing our path. Even though these are only momentary pauses, they are meditations nonetheless. We even do it in completely mundane ways; e.g., making a cup of tea. Yes! I kid you not! Think about that process for a moment. You know exactly how long to mash the teabag and how much milk to add. You've honed this action to perfection over the years and when you're making a cuppa, unless you're engaged in conversation at the time, you give it your complete focus for a few seconds. Teabag meditation! Looking at the sunset—sunset meditation! Watching a squirrel—squirrel meditation!

The point I'm making is that meditation isn't just a man-made technique developed by ancient sages living in caves. It's a natural process, just like those

Ultradian rhythms I described earlier. But although we're all born with an built-in ability to experience these meditative moments and can often enjoy them for long periods at a time as children, we tend to lose the knack of it as we grow up. In the same way that a body with stiff joints and muscles needs to exercise to help regain flexibility, so our minds also need exercise to help us get back to that childhood aptitude for blissful one-pointed focus. This is where a deeper, repetitive and more concentrated practise of meditation can help.

However, before I introduce you to this practise, let's look at a few very practical things you need to do before you begin.

Creating a Special Place

The first thing you need to do before embarking on any kind of meditation is to find a special place in your home that you can always use for this purpose. If you're lucky enough to have a spare room that can be turned over entirely to this practise, then go ahead and make it into your meditation room. Paint the walls a pale, tranquil shade or a neutral colour, have very little furniture in the room and keep the space as uncluttered as possible. A clear outer space leads to a clearer inner space. (You'll find out more on this in my chapter on "Clutter Clearing" in Part 2.) If you must have some pictures on the walls, only have a couple and it's best to choose ones which have a natural or contemplative theme.

If you're following a particular spiritual path, you may wish to place either a picture of your teacher or guru or an icon or representation of your chosen faith somewhere in the room. Alternatively, you might like to create a small altar with flowers, plants, candles, crystals, and any natural objects you've found, such as beautiful pebbles or feathers. Keep any other ornaments strictly limited to those associated with your meditational practise like tingshas (small cymbals used in Hindu and Buddhist worship), singing bowls, incense holders or bells, etc.

Make sure the room is well ventilated and heated and have a blanket or shawl to hand in case you become cold around the shoulders or feet. Choose a chair that suits you best for meditation purposes or put some cushions on the floor for seating.

Most of us however don't have the option of converting a room specifically for the practise of meditation, but that's not a problem. It can work just as well for you if you take time to choose a corner in your home that feels best for contemplation. You may need to try out several areas before you find your "spot". Once you've found it, use it every time. In doing so, you'll build up a special atmosphere there because the vibrations you produce whilst meditating will get stronger and support you in your practise.

Any small ritual you develop in association with meditation becomes grist to the mill in terms of getting you in the right frame of mind and mood. For example, it's nice to find some incense or joss sticks with a perfume that you like. Enjoy taking a little time to set these up and light them before you start your practise. Candlelight is also helpful (draw the curtains if you're burning candles during the day so you can benefit from the gentle flickering of their light).

Setting up some suitable music can also become part of your "ritual". There is a lot of meditation music around which many people find helpful, so you could find some CDs that you like. I always recommend the sound of Tibetan bells as background music as they can take people quite quickly into a deeper space within themselves. But it's all a matter of personal preference.

When to Meditate

Most people who meditate generally agree that first thing in the morning is the best time because this is when the mind is fresh and uncluttered with events of the day.

However, if you find that evenings or afternoons work better for you, then by all means do it then. But if you're doing it in the evening, it's best to do it before eating, as we're more prone to the possibility of falling asleep after a meal! The important thing is to try and establish a routine for meditating so that you'll be doing it each day at roughly the same time. This helps to get the body and mind into the habit of it. Once you've been practising for a while, you may well find there's a sense of something missing in your day if you haven't meditated.

Sitting Positions

You're going to be meditating for about 15 to 20 minutes so it's really important to choose a position that's *comfortable!* There's no point whatsoever in causing yourself unnecessary pain and discomfort because it will only get in the way of your concentration!

When you sit, it's important to keep your shoulders back with your spine straight and your head erect and centrally placed between your shoulders. Avoid leaning backwards against cushions or slouching forward with your head drooping down. An upright posture helps to maintain a state of alertness.

If you're supple enough to sit in the full lotus position (see Figure 1A, page 42), then go ahead. Otherwise either sit in the half lotus (see Figure 1B, page 42) or cross-legged position (see Figure 1C, page 43). If either of these poses are uncomfortable, you may find it easier to kneel on some cushions, with one

Figure 1A: The Full Lotus Pose

Figure 1B: The Half Lotus Pose

Model for all sitting positions: Bodel Rikys

Finding the River

Figure 1c: The Cross-Legged Pose

Figure 1d: The Kneeling Pose

big or a couple of small cushions tucked in underneath your bottom (see Figure 1D, page 43)or use one of the kneeling meditation stools that are available. If none of this works for you, then sit in a chair and place both feet firmly on the ground. Place your palms on your knees, or fold your hands in your lap.

The first technique I'm going to teach you is called "Following the Breath" (Exercise 14). This particular meditation helps us develop *mindfulness*, which is about becoming more aware of what's happening both within and outside of ourselves. It's also about living in the present moment. Learning to stay in the "now" can alleviate worry and anxiety, improve your concentration and help you to be more open and receptive. It will also help you enjoy those sunset, squirrel and tea bag meditations for longer!

In this meditation you're going to focus on your breath and try to let all other thoughts go. When your attention wanders (as it will!), simply acknowledge this has happened and firmly and gently bring your focus back again into your breathing process. This may happen many times, but don't worry! The mind is like a butterfly and flits from one thought and idea to another. What we're doing in this meditation is teaching it how to quiet down. It takes time to do this and some days are easier than others. Jack Kornfield, who is a well-known Buddhist teacher, psychologist and meditation master, says that the mind behaves like a puppy that is all over the place and into everything. That's a very good description! So, be as kind and good humoured with your wandering mind as you would be if you were training a puppy!

Please note: when I talk about "a breath" in this meditation, I mean one cycle of breath; i.e., one in-breath followed by one out-breath.

Exercise 14: Following the Breath

Take the phone off the hook, close the door to any animals, and tell anyone you're living with that you want to be left undisturbed for 15 to 20 minutes. You might like to have a clock or a watch with you so you can check when you need to stop. Alternatively, set the alarm on your mobile to indicate when time is up.

Put on your meditation music if you need it. Light your candles and your incense. Make sure you're comfortable and warm. Sit quietly in your chosen place and position. Close your eyes and bring your attention into your breathing process.

Notice how your breath passes in and out of your nostrils. Be aware of any sounds you make when you breathe through your nose. Stay with this for ten breaths. *(Remember, if your mind wanders, just acknowledge that it's happened and come back to focussing on your breathing again.)*

Now bring your attention downwards to the rise and fall of your chest. This automatic movement comes with each breath and is happening every moment of our lives even though we're rarely conscious of it. Observe this process for ten breaths.

Then bring your focus to the motion of the ribs swinging in and out—and give absolute attention to that for ten breaths.

Next, shift your concentration to the way the diaphragm pushes outwards and then pulls back when you breathe. Observe that for 10 breaths.

Finally, bring your awareness to the movement of your lower abdomen. Notice how it seems to open and close a little as it moves with each breath—and give your concentration to that for ten breaths.

Once you've completed this section, you're now free to focus on only *one* aspect of the breathing process (e.g., the passage of air through the nostrils, or the rise and fall of the chest, etc.), and stay focussed on that for the rest of your meditation time. Remember to bring your mind back to your breathing whenever it wanders!

When you've finished, keep your eyes closed and become aware of your *whole* body.

Feel the contact between your body and the chair or cushions you are sitting on. Notice the support and feel of any cushions you have propped up behind your back. If you're in a chair, be aware of the contact between your feet and the floor. Notice the feel of the carpet or floorboards beneath your feet.

Now give attention to the sounds in the room—the ticking of a clock, the creak of floorboards or noises from the rooms above. Become aware of sounds outside of the room—traffic, horns, people's voices or footsteps.

Finally, slowly and gently open your eyes and come back fully into the room. Stay sitting quietly for a while. Then notice how you're feeling, before standing up and getting on with your day.

Repeat this every day at the same time, if possible.

After you've done this meditation for a week or so, instead of going through all the aspects of your breathing process as above, you can go straight to focussing on only *one part of it*. Be sure to follow your breath for the full 15 to 20 minute meditation and remember to bring your mind back into focus when it gets hooked into something.

You may find your breathing slows naturally during this meditation. That's fine if it happens. **At no point should you actually try to change the rhythm of your natural breathing.**

With practise, you might feel you're able to extend your meditation time from 15 to 20 minutes into, say, 30 minutes, 45 minutes, or longer. It's up to you. Don't push yourself into this if it doesn't feel right. Build up the time gradually if you want to sit for longer.

When you've been doing this kind of meditation for a while, you may find you see colours, images or shapes. You might also become aware of a kind of light humming sound in your ears, which simply means you're hearing the sound of your own vibrations. This is all perfectly normal, so don't worry. (And don't worry if you don't notice any of these things!) We're all different and unique in the way we experience our meditations. Whatever you encounter, just observe it, acknowledge it and let it go as if watching clouds passing across the sky.

This meditation is helpful in bringing about a sense of inner one-ness, developing sharper clarity and perception and, most of all, for giving you that essential space to "press the pause button" each day.

A lot of people find it hard to maintain focus when they meditate. This is because of that puppy-dog mind, chasing around after everything it finds! Don't worry—it gets better the more you practise, but there is a traditional yoga technique for focussing and meditation which is very calming and it can help you with this. It's called Tratak (Exercise 15).

Exercise 15: Tratak

For this exercise, you're going to need a candle and a candlestick, and a low table where you can place the candle so the flame is on a *level with your eyes* when you sit down.

Having it on the same level as your eyes is very important, so you might need to experiment with where you're going to sit to ensure you're in the right position.

Make sure that the place you've chosen is quiet and that you'll be undisturbed for the next 15 to 20 minutes. Don't sit anywhere there's going to be a draught and have a shawl close by to keep you warm if you feel you need it.

Choose a meditation posture which isn't difficult. You don't want to be distracted by an uncomfortable body while you're doing this! When you're settled and ready to begin, close your eyes and spend a few moments following your breath as per the previous exercise.

Now, open your eyes and gaze at the flame for a few seconds and then close your eyes again. Try to keep the image of the flame in your mind's eye as clearly as you can. Visualise its brightness, the shape of it, and the size of its "halo" (the glowing circle around the flame).

Whenever the image fades (as it will), open your eyes and repeat the whole process of gazing at the flame for a few seconds before closing your eyes again. Keep doing this as many times as feels comfortable. When thoughts intrude, just acknowledge them and bring your attention back into gazing at the flame.

Do this exercise fairly frequently in the early days of meditation. It will help your concentration and ability to visualise. When you've been practising it for a while, you should find you don't have to stare at the flame for too long before you can hold its image in your mind. Eventually, you'll be able to conjure the image of a flame without sitting in front of a candle.

This exercise should also help you to find some more stillness inside.

Finding the River

The final meditation technique I'm going to introduce you to is another mindfulness practise, but this is a walking meditation (Exercise 16). Moving meditations are often more appealing for those of us who tend to be busy, busy, busy all the time doing two or more things at once; e.g., watching TV or reading while you eat or checking your emails while you're on the phone!

You do this meditation with your eyes open and it's a great way of being active and calming the mind at the same time. Once you've got the hang of it, it can be beautifully combined with walking in Nature and allowing some fresh air to fill your lungs.

Exercise 16: Walking Meditation

Find a space in your home or garden where you can walk back and forth unobstructed for about 10 to 15 steps. Clear a space in a room in order to do this if necessary. You can walk in a continuous circle if it's easier, but don't make the circle too small otherwise you might end up feeling a bit dizzy! Do whatever is easiest according to the space you have available.

Start by taking off your shoes and standing quietly with your arms hanging loosely at your sides. Bring your focus into your breathing for a few moments (see Exercise 14, page 44) to help centre yourself.

Then turn your attention down into the soles of your feet and really feel the connection between the feet and the floor. Allow your feet and toes to stretch out completely so that the whole of the foot is connected to the ground. This stimulates all your nerves, arteries and meridians or subtle energy pathways (more about these in Part 2.) Notice the texture of the floor or the surface beneath you. Feel the weight of your body being taken by the soles of your feet. Allow that. Become aware of how the floor is supporting the entire weight of your body. Allow that, too. You may find that your body feels heavier when you do this. That's good! It means you're relaxing and grounding. Stay with this sensation for a few moments.

When you feel ready, bring your hands together in front of you and fold them over your diaphragm. Direct your gaze downwards to a few feet in front of you.

Now, start to walk as though you were in slow motion. Very slowly, prise one foot off the ground and place it with great focus in front of the other. Then do the same with the other foot. Keep doing this and move v-e-r-y slowly! Whilst walking, bring all of your attention into the feeling and movements of your feet and toes. You may find that you're walking with a slightly rolling motion from side to side and feel a bit wobbly at first.

Just as you did in the previous meditation, when thoughts arise (as they will!), simply notice and acknowledge them and then bring your attention back into your slow walking. Again, you may have to do this many times, but that's OK. Just remember you're training the puppy!

Do this meditation for about 15 to 20 minutes for 3 or 4 days. Practise in the confines of your home or garden to get used to the idea of focussing on your feet. Little by little, you can allow yourself to walk a tiny bit faster until you're less "slow motion" and more "slow walking".

Then you can try putting on your shoes and going out into the local park or countryside and doing it. Put your hands in your pockets and walk slowly and with great awareness in your feet for as long as you can. *Never* allow yourself to speed up to your normal pace of walking. As with the previous meditation, you can build up the time you spend on this and make it longer if you wish. It brings the same benefits as "Following the Breath".

By the way, if you find you like doing a moving meditation, you might be interested in looking for some local Qi Gong or Tai Chi classes, as these practises are also forms of moving meditation. They are equally calming and beneficial for your health.

Troubleshooting

Sleepiness: If you find you're getting sleepy during the sitting meditation and dropping off, try opening your eyes a little and directing your gaze downwards to a place a few feet in front of you. Then continue with your mediation. If this doesn't help, try switching to the Walking Meditation.

Restlessness: This is often linked with boredom or a sense that "nothing is happening". The mind jumps around and keeps pulling you away from your focus. Just acknowledge it and then bring your focus back to your breathing or walking.

Aversion: This is when you find pressing things to do that you tell yourself are *far* more important than your meditation practise. *Everyone* goes through this from time to time, including me! Be aware of what's happening and recognise it for what it is. Try coaxing yourself back into it by telling yourself you'll only sit or walk for 5 minutes. You may find you're able to extend this time once you get started.

Remember: cultivate a benign and kindly attitude towards yourself. Be patient. Doing this for yourself will also help with your attitude towards others!

Don't worry if you think you're not making any progress or that it's not working. Meditation isn't a technique that magically blanks out the mind and takes you straight into profound contemplation! It can't be measured in the way that you'd measure exercising where persistent practise visibly shows a greater suppleness and you can actually feel a build-up in strength. *No such markers exist with meditation practise.* As Jack Kornfield says, "Meditation has its seasons," so be prepared to experience changeable weather!

When you meditate you become very aware of how your mind attaches itself to various things. It is constantly butterflying from one thought to another. If you're troubled and distressed you'll notice the mind will intrude with endless thoughts about the issues in hand. Happy thoughts can also be an intrusion! This is perfectly normal. Again, acknowledge the thoughts and return to focus on your breathing. Bringing the mind back is like calling a puppy to heel.

Finally, if these meditations lead you towards wanting to deepen your practise, see if you can find some meditation classes in your area. It's really helpful to have a teacher in the early days and it's also very encouraging to meditate in a class with others (see Resources and Suggested Reading at the back of the book).

Chapter 7
A Part of Something Greater: The Practice of Spirituality

People often get confused about the word "spirituality", thinking it means believing in a specific religion. That's not true. There are some folk who don't follow any religion at all but who are deeply spiritual nevertheless. Such people have found their own way of expressing their beliefs, often through a blend of understandings drawn from various sources and personal experience.

Some people also make the mistake of thinking that becoming "spiritual" means they don't have to deal with the darker sides of their nature. A number of spiritual teachings encourage an intense focus on our higher aspects at the expense of ignoring the more basic levels of our being. Any problems relating to hang ups, negative attitudes, money, sex and relationships, etc., don't magically disappear when you start exploring your spirituality!

You see, any kind of spiritual unfolding is a process that is rather like building a house. The foundation has to be dug and laid before the construction can rise up out of the dust. And how do we get to have firm foundations? By becoming aware of our problems and difficulties and being prepared to work on them as required. That way, they're less likely to jump out and push us off balance!

It's a strange paradox, but the more we aspire to higher consciousness, the more we may encounter what is known as our "shadow" (a term describing the murkier side of ourselves which isn't all sweetness and light)! Maybe you have come across instances of this already? For example, it shows up when people appear highly spiritual or deeply religious on the surface, but underneath they're actually very critical and judgemental, or pompous, arrogant and "holier than thou". This kind of attitude sneaks up on people and takes them unawares. It comes about through not being conscious of faults and projecting personal imperfections onto others.

Working on ourselves is therefore even more important if we want to explore our spiritual nature. If we only focus on our higher aspects and pay no attention to the lower ones, we're de-stabilising the structure of "the building". It's hard to see this happening when we're in the middle of the process, but it usually shows up through our attitudes and behaviour to others.

Everything we've covered so far in this book has been about basic understandings of body, mind and emotions, beginning to work with these levels, and learning ways to deal with stress and challenges. All this paves the way to exploring your spirituality—if you want to.

You've seen how your mind, body and emotions are interlinked and have begun to learn ways to keep them in balance. This helps towards gaining physical, mental and emotional well-being, which in turn supports your spiritual practise. As you develop your higher consciousness, it brings yourself and everything around you into a sense of connection and oneness. Increasing that level of consciousness helps you to live more in the present moment, and being in the here and now means there's less worry and anxiety. With this comes a greater sense of well-being which helps you to be more grounded and centred. Round and round. No part of you functions in isolation because everything is connected to everything else. Nothing is separate. It's all part of *one whole thing!*

But if you're seeking a way into spirituality and don't seem to be getting anywhere, where do you start?

Well, you may have already begun without knowing it.

Have you ever experienced a moment or time in your life where you found yourself doing something or being somewhere—perhaps out in Nature—and in that moment, everything seemed to be in flow? When out of the blue you suddenly felt the most incredible sense of peace and tranquillity? When you felt completely aligned with the Universe and that all was well in your world?

These blissful sensations are the very same feelings which have been described in just about every spiritual tradition as mystical or religious experiences. For thousands of years we've been told that these states are encounters with God/the Divine/the Supreme Consciousness/the One/the Universe—or whichever term you might choose to describe the essence or centre of existence.

Any experience of this nature is in fact yet another totally natural occurrence and most of us have had one at some point in our lives. These events don't necessarily have any connection to traditional religions. They can happen to people from all walks of life, race, colour, creed or persuasion. And you don't have to belong to a particular faith or religion to experience them. They can even happen to people who don't have any spiritual leanings at all!

The commencement of one's spiritual journey often begins this way. Mystical or meaningful events don't tend to come in the form of some great bolt of lightning blasting down from the sky. They appear more frequently from a sudden opening of the heart, or a sense of stillness, peace and belonging.

These blissful sensations are openings or gateways into our spirituality and they can be triggered by all manner of things. They can arise through anything from music, dancing, and drumming to enjoying a peak sexual experience. They can come from being inside the awesome majesty of some great building or admiring the staggering beauty of a natural landscape. They can arise from extraordinary psychic or telepathic happenings or noticing synchronicities and co-incidences. They can occur during or after tragic situations, suffering and distress. They can also come through a sense of contact with some beloved person who has passed on or through channelling an inner guide. And they can, of course, also arise through earnest prayer and deep meditation.

Recognising these "gateways to bliss" is important, for if you're not already aligned to some spiritual practise, they're a very good starting point for you. Calling them to mind as often as possible can be very helpful.

If you've ever had one of those blissful moments of awe and wonder, Exercise 17 will help you build on the experience.

Exercise 17: Gateway Meditation

Spend a few moments following your breath and coming into your body.

Choose a special moment you recall that you identify as a "gateway to bliss". Bring it back to mind with all the intensity you can muster. Really see the colours and the light. Hear the sounds. Feel the feelings. Remember the experience of connection and oneness it brought to you.

Notice the sensations you feel. Open your heart to them. Appreciate them and give thanks for this experience. Allow it to penetrate and melt into every part of your being—bones, muscles, cells, organs, brain. Breathe it in.

Let yourself float in it. Bathe in it. Be with it. Spend time in it. Soak it up! You may find that for brief moments, all thoughts disappear.

Stay with this for about 15 to 20 minutes, or as long as you can.

Then slowly bring your attention back into the room and feel the connection between your body and where you are sitting. Become aware of the sounds in the room. Open your eyes gently and stay sitting for a short while afterwards, reflecting on what you've just experienced.

Exercise 17 is by William Bloom.

This is a good way of anchoring these feelings. Do it often. Use other similar experiences in the same way.

If you haven't had any blissful experiences, just take yourself back to "Creating a Safe Place Within Yourself" (page 5) or to "The Connection", (page 7). Choose whichever feels most powerful and practise it often. Don't have any preconceived ideas about where it might take you. Just let it unfold and, above all, enjoy it!

That feeling of connection and belonging is enormously comforting and gives us a sense of being part of something else. It can provide welcome inner support and much comfort. In times of crisis, it's a well-researched fact that people with spiritual beliefs often tend to cope better with challenges than those without any. When logic doesn't provide any answers, spiritual beliefs and understandings can bring solace and meaning to difficult times.

Exercise 18 is a meditation to help in times of trouble, whether it be trauma or crisis or lesser problems. It immediately links you with those blissful moments we've already encountered, and helps you to find strength and uplift. It's adapted from a very ancient practise that comes from Tibet.

Exercise 18: Uplifting and Unburdening the Heart

Begin by going back in your mind to the gateway that gave you the greatest sense of connection to bliss. Imagine yourself there, quiet and peaceful. Allow yourself to feel the full experience of uplift and oneness it gave you. As best you can, according to your emotional state at the time, allow those blissful feelings to soak into you.

Now imagine a brilliant blue summer sky above the scene you're remembering. Bring into it a representation of the Divine or the Universe or anything which you feel embodies the essence of that connection. This could be a religious figure like Jesus, Mary, the Buddha or Krishna, etc. If this doesn't feel right for whatever reason, don't worry. Instead, bring to mind an image of the sun or a star or a cloud of light, or some other powerful image that feels appropriate.

Whatever you choose, know that you've invoked an image which is totally benevolent, compassionate, loving and healing. Open your heart to it and tell it all your troubles. Describe everything that's giving you pain, anxiety and distress. Pour out your heart to it. Don't hold back. You won't be judged for *anything* you might say.

As you start speaking or praying to this image, visualise it giving out a stream of radiant white light. Know that this light is both transforming and healing. Know that its power is immense and can heal and purify you from any kind of block, difficulty, trauma, or crisis.

Imagine this radiant light becoming brighter and more brilliant the more you unburden yourself.

Imagine this light pouring into the crown of your head and streaming down inside, filling up every part of you with its brilliance. Imagine it washing out all your troubles and pain. As you keep asking for help and guidance, the blazing light may eventually cascade over you like a great waterfall.

Continue telling it all your woes until you begin to feel a sense of peace descending

---

upon you. As this happens, allow yourself to relax and feel the bliss of this great love and healing you're receiving.

Allow yourself to melt into the embrace of this love. Then imagine you're able to lift yourself effortlessly off the ground and float up into that great blue summer sky and meet that image you chose. Imagine yourself embracing that image. If it's a figure, see yourself curled up in its lap, head against its shoulder, enfolded in its arms. If you chose the sun or a beautiful star, imagine yourself curled up comfortably and safely in its centre, enfolded in its loving and gentle light. Stay there for as long as you need.

Come back slowly and gently into your body. Sit for a while and take stock of how you're feeling. Notice how it feels in your head. Notice how it feels in your heart. Notice how it feels in your belly. Don't be in a hurry to get back into everyday things.

Exercise 18 is derived from a meditation described by Andrew Harvey in his book *The Direct Path*.

Use this exercise whenever you need it. The more you practise it, the easier it becomes. After you've established how much it can help, and you can access it quite easily, you can develop a shortened version of it for lesser problems. In this case, take yourself directly to the image you chose and allow its light to pour into you as you tell it your problems. Then, as soon as you've finished unburdening yourself, rise up towards it and become enfolded within its healing presence. This meditation can teach you trust in a higher power. It can help you find solace and relief from all difficulties and sorrows whenever you wish.

The longer version is particularly powerful and helpful in times of great distress.

If you've already established a spiritual practise and have been meditating for some time, you may have found that every now and again thoughts disappear for a moment or two and you slip into a kind of gap in your consciousness. In these small spaces, there's no sense of the passage of time. Twenty minutes may feel like only five. You may also find you're experiencing something subtly different about yourself.

At these points, you could have a sense of what Deepak Chopra describes as the place, "...where 'me' and 'not me' peacefully co-exist within the same mind." We sometimes get a sense of this in ordinary life. It usually happens quite out of the blue. You might be engaged in doing something when quite suddenly there's a part of you that's like a fly on the wall, watching yourself. Have you ever had that happen to you?

Well, this is an occurrence that is found much more frequently in meditation practises. And it's a valuable inborn ability that is well worth developing. It's the part of us that is naturally able to be quiet, still, detached, observant and utterly NOW. This aspect of ourselves is known as "The Witness".

Exercise 19 is a meditation technique which helps you to develop that "witness" ability.

Exercise 19: Moon, Lake, Reflection Meditation

Close your eyes and follow your breath for long enough to quiet yourself and become centred and in your body.

Now imagine that it is night time, and you're sitting beside a calm, peaceful lake in the moonlight. See the lake in your mind's eye.

See a bright silver crescent moon shining above the lake in the night sky.

Now turn your attention to the reflection of the moon in the water, and put all your focus into looking at that for about 5 minutes.

Imagine you are *watching yourself* doing this. You're watching yourself beside the lake looking at the reflection of the moon in the water. Give this all your focus and attention. Stay with this for about 5 minutes.

Now, ask yourself this question, "Who is watching and who is meditating? Is it the meditator who watches? Is it the watcher who meditates?"

Contemplate these questions.

As you do this, switch back and forth between the meditator and the watcher and spend around 3 to 5 minutes with each of them. Keep doing this for a little until you naturally find your focus settling down to either your contemplation of the question or watching yourself watching the reflection of the moon. Stay with this until your meditation time is up (around 15 to 20 minutes—or longer if it happens that way).

Slowly come back into the room and into your body. Breathe and stretch and wiggle you hands, fingers, toes and feet. Note how you're feeling in mind and body and don't be in a hurry to move.

Keep repeating this exercise every few days for about a month. It's helping you learn how to become reflective, still and contemplative. It also increases your self-awareness. Go back to it whenever these qualities need strengthening.

You can take this meditation out into your everyday life in pleasant, easy ways. For example, watch the reflection of a sunset on the waves, or light dancing on the waters of a pond in your local park. Ask yourself: Who is watching you doing this? Alternatively, when you wake up after remembering a dream, ask yourself who was watching the dreamer dream?

Spirituality is a vast subject and I can only brush the surface of it here. In the space available, all I can provide is a brief overview, a few guidelines and meditations, and a glimpse of how this level of our being completes the overall picture of our human potential.

I hope the following suggestions will also be useful for helping you on way:

- Be guided by your instinct. If you're drawn to something, investi it. If you find someone who sounds like an interesting teacher, go along and hear what they have to say. Take your time before you make a commitment to anyone or anything.

- Don't forget to look around at other things as well. Try to develop an overview.

- Be prepared for the fact that spiritual matters may not always give you the clear answers you're expecting. Giving yourself permission to *not know* sometimes can help you remain open.

- Remember that personal and spiritual growth happens on lots of different levels. Sometimes it may feel as though it's all happening at once and sometimes you may think it isn't happening at all! But I promise you, something is always happening on some level. Remember, for each person, it's an utterly unique and individual process. Don't compare yourself with others!

- Don't forget how important it is to deal with the nitty-gritty of your emotions. As William Bloom says, "If you don't consciously manage your emotions then your emotions will manage you!"

Spirituality doesn't have to be "other-worldly." Any spiritual practises you choose to do can become part of your daily life. Even meditation can turn into a routine as normal as cleaning your teeth!

Watch out for any teachers who give you the impression they have all the answers. Believe me, *no one* has all the answers! Some spiritual teachers tend to set themselves above ordinary folk. And whilst they may have a lot of knowledge and be very wise, please remember they are human beings just like you and me!

Teachers who are able to display transparency about their own shortcomings and challenges are a real plus!

There's a difference between wanting to become deeply embedded in your spirituality and just being interested in it. You have the choice! If you're really serious, then you need to practise daily until it becomes part of your everyday life and rhythm. It's like learning to use a computer! You'll never get the hang of it unless you sit down and work with it and learn all the commands and techniques! You don't have to live in a cave, but you do have to be prepared to make a commitment.

Let your spiritual practise be part of your life. I don't mean that you have to become obsessive, monk-like or evangelical. It's perfectly possible to express your spirituality in a calm, open-hearted and gentle way. It can help you to access inner peace, trust a higher power, develop a compassionate attitude towards yourself and others, and feel connected, grounded and part of something greater.

OM SHANTI, SHANTI, SHANTI

Peace, peace, peace

Part II

Everything Is Energy

Chapter 8

Bliss Fields, Energy Pathways, and Star Stuff

The first understandings about the energetic relationship between life and the Universe happened thousands of years ago in ancient India and China. Not surprisingly, this knowledge didn't come about through the use of scientific experiments or special instruments, but through the sages and seers of the time attaining profound levels in meditation.

You see, with regular and disciplined practise, it's possible to reach a point in meditation where waves of deep peace or fields of bliss can be felt moving in and around the physical body. Adepts from almost every kind of spiritual discipline attest to the existence of these fields that became known by different names across the cultures. In India it was called Prana. In China it was known as Chi or Qi. And in the West, it became known as Universal Energy or Subtle Energy.

The ancient sages and rishis (holy men) of India explored these energy fields through long periods of contemplation and meditation, and in so doing came to understand that this energy permeated everything, including the planet we live upon and the Universe itself. They saw these fields to be the cosmic breath of life that was breathed by the Universe, infusing everything with its subtle energy. Through their perception of the existence of Chi, they divined the human being's intrinsic connection to all things. This meant that, in essence, there was no difference between man and the animals, a rock or a plant, or between nature and the sun, moon and stars.

This knowledge teaches us that we are part and parcel of the cosmos and the idea that "we are all made from the same star stuff" (as Richard Gerber says in his book *Vibrational Medicine*) is pretty mind-boggling, isn't it? For left-brained, science-driven people, the concept is mostly unacceptable and cultures in the West dismissed this knowledge as a figment of the mystic imagination for hundreds of years. And so it wasn't until the beginning of the 20th century when Einstein's famous equation of $E = mc^2$ proved that absolutely everything, from a grain of sand to a human being, is made up of particles of electric energy interacting with electromagnetic fields.

Einstein and his peers were pioneers in a brand new field of science called Quantum Physics. Their findings rocked the foundations of previously held Newtonian thought that saw the universe as ordered, disciplined and behaving in nicely predictable ways. Suddenly, we had quantum theories showing us an extraordinary world of simultaneous chaos and order, a world where energy shape-shifted and behaved in all manner of extraordinary ways. Gary Zukav describes this beautifully in his book *The Dancing Wu Li Masters*, "… the world (is composed of) …sparkling energy forever dancing with itself in the form of its particles as they twinkle in and out of existence, collide, transmute and disappear again."

Don't worry! I'm not going to lead you into an exploration of Particle Physics! (I couldn't take you there even if I tried!), but what this all boils down to are a couple of basic facts about energy which are very interesting:

- First, to quote Fritjof Capra in his book *The Tao of Physics*, "Quantum theory reveals….(that)…..as we penetrate into matter, nature does not show us any isolated 'basic building blocks' but rather appears as a complicated web of relations between the various parts of the whole." In other words, the discoveries of modern physics imply that *everything* is interwoven, and we are all part of the same thing. This highlights a fascinating and unexpected relationship between Eastern mysticism (All is One and One is All) and modern scientific thought.

- Second, what's considered to be solid matter is actually made up of atoms that then break down into microscopic particles. For example, a chair or a table aren't solid matter at all, but vibrations of energy which have taken on a solid appearance. As Dr Richard Gerber says in *Vibrational Medicine* "…all matter is energy and light in its myriad forms and manifestations." In other words, the ancient sages were right!

If everything is energy, then we have to accept that the same is true of the home in which you live, the roads and pavements, your car, the lawn mower, a supermarket trolley, your pet dog or cat, Big Ben, your TV, computer and mobile and anything else you can think of—including your body!

You might find it hard to think of your body as lots of bits of energy but that's exactly what it is. Deepak Chopra explained this perfectly when he said, "We tend to see our bodies as 'frozen sculptures'—solid, fixed, material objects—when in truth they are more like rivers, constantly flowing patterns of intelligence."

We have to thank those amazing Indian rishis and sages again for perceiving that we are more than a dense amalgamation of flesh, muscles and bones. For in addition to their understandings about the nature of life and the universe, they were also able to perceive clairvoyantly that we had a subtle energetic anatomy—a sort of ethereal counterpart to the manifestation of our physical bodies—that was nourished by the cosmic breath of Chi. This body, known as the Energy Body or Subtle Body, is an exact replica of the physical body, but instead of holding vital organs and various bodily systems, it's made up of non-physical energy centres, pathways and circuits along which the subtle energy of Chi flows.

What these Eastern mystics realised was that energy pathways (which they called the Nadis) criss-crossed all over the energy body. They also perceived that numbers of Nadis converge at various points along a central line of the body extending from the base of the torso to the crown of the head. They identified these meeting points as energy centres and called them the Chakras (meaning wheels) because they constantly spin and turn. As they rotate, they pull in the subtle energy of the Universe (the Chi) that is then distributed out into the physical body via the Nadis.

They also perceived that there was an electromagnetic field around the human body (and indeed, around all living organisms), which they called the Aura. This is described as an egg-shaped, multi-layered sphere of energy that is generated by the spinning of the Chakras. It extends beyond the physical body to a distance of 2 to 4 feet—sometimes more—depending on the health, vitality and spiritual evolvement of the person.

These understandings of the subtle energy body formed the basis of the Indian medical system which is called Ayurveda (meaning Science of Life). Ayurveda is a completely holistic practise for the enhancement of life and spiritual unfoldment. It encompasses not only the concepts of the subtle energy system and how it works, but yoga, herbal medicine, a detailed understanding of the human body types and constitutions, diet guidelines, therapeutic treatments for all ailments, and meditation. Their mapping of the subtle energy body with its centres and pathways is more complex than the one I've outlined above, but there are plenty of books around which can give you further information on this if you are interested (see Further Information and Suggested Reading at the back of the book).

The knowledge of Ayurveda was shared with Tibet, which had a similar medical system, and it spread to China through visits from pilgrims and traders. Here, it was integrated into the Chinese system of medicine (Traditional Chinese Medicine or TCM for short) and developed further according to their own understandings. Under the Chinese system, the Nadis became known as the Meridians and less emphasis was placed on the Chakras than in the Ayurvedic model. Instead, the Chinese chose to focus more on the meridians, and in particular, a loop of energy or meridian line in the body, that they call the Microcosmic Circuit. This is an energy line that runs vertically round and round the body moving from a point under the groin, up the back of the spine, over the top of the head, down the centre of the front of the body (through all the Chakras) and back to the groin again (Figure 2 clarifies the direction in which the energy moves).

You might like to try Exercise 20 to help you get in touch with this energy circuit.

Exercise 20: Sensing Your Inner Energy

Look at the diagram of the Microcosmic Circuit in Figure 2. Notice the direction of its flow that runs up the back and down the front of the body in a never-ending circle.

The visualisation I'm going to teach you can be done standing, sitting or lying down, so you can choose whatever position you prefer. When you're ready, close your eyes and come into your breath. Spend some time following the breath and calming your body and mind. Take whatever time you need to get yourself into a nice relaxed place in yourself.

Now bring your attention to an area about the width of two fingers below the navel. Place your hand there and use your fingers to measure it and make sure you're in the right place. Let your lower finger press lightly into this place to concentrate your mind on this area. This is an energetic space within you which is known in Chinese as the Dantien and in Japanese as the Hara. (Because I've always known it as the Hara, that's the name I'll be using to refer to it.) Keep in mind where the Hara is, as it's an important place to know about and I'll be talking about it again in other chapters.

Now bring your attention back to the Microcosmic Circuit. Imagine you can see this energetic "ring road" inside of you. You might like to imagine a small bead of golden light travelling round and round this circuit to help you in your visualisation.

Begin imagining your Chi travelling round and round your body—under your groin, up your spine, over the top of your head, down the centre of your front and under the groin—and round and round and round again.

Do this several times at your own speed, but don't go too fast. Do 5 to 6 circuits. Enjoy getting a sense of your energy moving around within you.

When you're ready to finish doing this exercise, bring your energy down the centre of your body for the last time and let it come to rest in your Hara. Place both palms on this area as if you were a pregnant woman feeling your precious, unborn child.

Be aware of how it feels in this area. Spend a bit of time there. Being in your Hara is very grounding and a great way to centre yourself.

Exercise 20 is an endorphin exercise by William Bloom.

Consciously moving energy around the Microcosmic Circuit like this and allowing the Chi to collect in the Hara (explained in Exercise 20) can improve

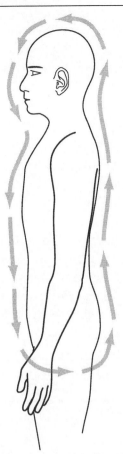

health and vitality. The practise of Tai Chi and Qi Gong place a lot of focus on these areas.

The Hara is seen to be the energetic centre of gravity in the human body and the seat of one's inner Chi. Have you ever seen those statues of Buddhas with big round bellies? Well, those pot bellies aren't meant to imply the Buddhas are a bit greedy and eat too much food. They actually represent Buddhas who are very powerful because they've got large amounts of Chi in their bellies!

Chi is a substance without physical form, so it can't be seen by the naked eye. The subtle energy body isn't detectable through x-rays or microscopes, although it has always been seen by those with clairvoyant eyesight, so you won't be surprised to hear that, for a very long time, the West—with its "prove-it-to-me-otherwise-I-won't-believe-it" mind set—dismissed these ideas as mumbo jumbo for hundreds of years.

It wasn't until the 1940s when the scientists Valentin and Semyon Kirlian (a husband and wife team) discovered how to take photographs of this energy, that credence was finally given to its existence. This photographic method became known as Kirlian Photography and you'll find demonstrations of this technique at most Mind and Body Exhibitions these days. Further scientific evidence was provided in the 1970s, when Dr Valerie Hunt of UCLA University confirmed the existence of coloured energetic emanations from the Chakras and the Aura which could give an indication of the health and wellbeing of the individual.

Now, if you've never come across any of this information before, or you've heard about it but always thought it was a bit flaky, you may be finding it hard to get a handle on any of this. Either way, let me reassure you that it's all a lot more accessible than it might seem at first. First and foremost, the good news is that you don't have to be a saintly meditation adept living in a cave to experience these waves of energy. Why? Because you can get a very good sense of them every time you trigger your endorphins and have a joyful, blissful or ecstatic experience! So, if you've done the earlier exercises, you're already on your way to getting a feel for all of this.

The second bit of good news is that you don't have to be a psychic or a healer to be able to *feel* this energy in tangible ways! Exercise 21 shows you how easy it is to feel your own energy field with a little bit of practise.

Exercise 21: Feeling Your Own Aura

Rub your hands together briskly so they become very warm. Now, using your dominant hand, very slowly bring the palm of that hand towards the back of the other one, getting closer and closer all the time.

You may feel a subtle resistance in the palm of your dominant hand as it approaches the back of the other one.

What you're feeling is your own aura.

Another way to do this is to again rub the hands together very vigorously. Then hold the hands about 18 inches apart and slowly—very slowly—bring both palms together. You may experience a kind of bouncy feeling as though you've got some invisible balloon between the two hands. If you don't feel this at first, draw your hands apart and slowly move them back towards each other again. Keep doing this until you feel that resistance I've described above.

If you haven't got it yet, keep practising and you will. It will suddenly come to you and you'll wonder why you didn't feel it before.

Exercise 22 explains another way for you to feel an aura, but you'll need a friend to help you with this one:

Exercise 22: Feeling Someone Else's Aura

First, do some body movements to loosen yourself up. Do some dancing or jump up and down. Or shake out your arms and your feet. Imagine you've got some chewing gum stuck on the ends of your fingers and toes and pretend that you're trying to flick it off. Or imagine you're a dog that's been for a dip in the sea and has come out wanting to shake all that water out of its fur. Go on! *Shake!* Shake yourself from top to toe. Do it several times.

Now, have your friend stand still and go and stand about 4 to 5 feet away, Extend your palms outwards with them facing towards your friend. Now, v-e-r-y slowly, start walking towards that person. As you get closer, you may feel that subtle resistance in your hands again or a sense that the air is thickening around them.

That's you feeling your friend's aura!

You might like to try feeling the energy field of different things like trees and plants and animals in the same way. The more you practise, the more sensitive your hands will become.

Now, let's take all this a few steps further.

Do you remember how, in Chapter 2, we looked at how the body and mind are linked? In light of what I've been explaining so far, it therefore follows that if the *body* is composed of energy, then the *mind* must also be composed of energy. And if the mind is energy then your *thoughts* are energy, too!

Thoughts are waves of energy. They radiate in all directions and are constantly transmitted and received by yourself and others. Every time you think a thought you're firing off a small bolt of energy. Thoughts produce vibrations which continue to pulsate even after you've forgotten what you were thinking. Thoughts build up atmospheres that, sometimes, can actually be felt. Some thought vibrations, depending on their strength, can last for centuries!

To demonstrate this, work through Exercise 23.

Exercise 23: Sensing Energies in Rooms and Buildings

Go back in your mind for a moment and recall a time when you've been in a room where people were having an argument. Try to remember what the atmosphere in that room felt like.

When we walk into a room or experience an environment full of tension and bad feeling we talk about how you can cut the atmosphere with a knife. This is because the kind of energies released by anger, resentment and rage are so thick and dense they feel tangible. When an argument has taken place, the vibrations in that room are completely imbued with a fiery, toxic, energetic discharge.

OK. Pause and take a breath. Breathe out that unpleasant sensation you've recalled. Do this a few times if it still feels uncomfortable.

Now switch modes. Think of some great cathedral or temple you've visited, preferably one which is still in use. If you don't have a memory of a cathedral or temple, instead bring to mind when you were in a room where people practised meditation, or when you visited your local church or some similar place of worship. Take a few moments to recall the atmosphere.

You'll almost certainly feel that this time, the place you've chosen to recall, contains much lighter vibrations of peace and calm which may cause you to feel quiet and reflective. That's because it is filled with the energy of prayer which has been created by worshippers who have visited that place for years—sometimes centuries. The longer similar thoughts and energies have been released into an atmosphere, the more they build up and the stronger they become.

Both the atmospheres described in Exercise 23 were created through energy and thought.

Thought follows energy and energy follows thought.
As we think, so we create

Thoughts are amazingly powerful. Do you remember how, in Exercise 4 (page 9), you recalled an unpleasant incident that caused uncomfortable feelings and memories to return? And do you remember how in Exercise 1 (page 4) and Exercise 2 (page 5), happy, enjoyable memories of being out in Nature created a sense of well-being within you? Both these exercises were demonstrations of energy following thought. You created something by thinking about it. Be very careful about the kind of thoughts and energies you link into because, as we've seen with these exercises, they can have a direct effect on your mental and emotional state.

Just as eating a healthy, balanced diet is good for our physical bodies, so we need to ensure that we're feeding wisely in terms of energy. You see, whatever we give attention to mentally, emotionally and spiritually can be seen as "food". We've already seen how negative thoughts don't do us any good in terms of the hormones they release. Well, they don't benefit us energetically, either. Feeding on worry and negativity is the equivalent of existing on a diet of junk food! So it follows that when you make yourself feel good by thinking about a happy time or doing something you enjoy, you're feeding yourself very healthy and nourishing food. It's therefore extremely important to pay attention to the kind of energies we're feeding on in all areas of life—the environment you live in, the places you frequent, the books you read, the people you mix with, the films you see, the music you listen to, etc. All these things provide food on an energetic level. When we talk about food in this way it's called *energy nutrition*. So, watch what you're taking in, because the wrong foods can give us energetic indigestion!

We're nearing the end of this brief exploration of how we're all energetic beings connected to everything else in a Universe entirely composed of energy. But there's just one more aspect of the subtle fields we haven't yet covered. Chi also flows through our planet Earth, and through our environment, and we need to see how that affects us too.

Everything in the Universe has its own magnetic field. This means that bodies like the sun and the stars and the Earth emit huge energy fields. The ancient sages divined that powerful currents of Chi flowed within the Earth's aura that were believed to move along paths that criss-cross the planet, sometimes for hundreds of miles. In the West, these lines of energy are called Ley Lines and they are the Earth's meridians.

Many early sites of worship were built and aligned to these earth meridians. These areas have always been connected with increased levels of earth energy and were used extensively by our pagan ancestors as places of healing and areas where sacred ceremonies were performed. The ancient Celts"...perfected an art of living in harmony with the land that recognised the creative Life Force that animated it."*

Sometimes, circles of huge standing stones were built upon these lines, as in Stonehenge and Avebury in England. These were constructed in order to concentrate the Earth Energy and then spiral it out into the surrounding countryside. As Christianity spread slowly throughout the British Isles, pagan practises were forbidden but continued in secret. Sacred sites were razed to the ground and churches erected in their place, often with the full knowledge of the powerful energies running through the earth beneath them.

These terrestrial flows of energy are seen to be important for the health, well-being and good fortune of the human race, and the ancient science of Feng Shui arose out of detailed studies of this concept. Maintaining a free and even flow of Chi through our homes and environment is just as important as clearing obstacles to it within our subtle Energy Body. Blockages in both areas can cause difficulties in all parts of our lives.

There are ways of accessing the Chi within us to manage challenges, negative thoughts and emotions, our physical well-being and our environment. This can be achieved through using techniques which have been developed through Energy Psychology, Energy Exercises, Energy Medicine and Feng Shui, and we're going to be looking at some of the ways you can work with these methods in the following chapters.

---

* From *The Sun and the Serpent* by Hamish Miller and Paul Broadhurst

Chapter 9

Clearing Clutter and Enhancing the Chi in your Home

Have you ever noticed the way you sometimes get an immediate sense of how you resonate with a place as soon as you walk in through the front door? A really good example of this often happens during house hunting. It's as though we've got antennae! We can tune into the vibrations of the house we're viewing and know immediately whether it's right or wrong for us.

This is because rooms and houses soak up the thoughts and vibrations of those who live in them. Emotional energies become embedded in the walls. These have been unconsciously generated not only by the people who live there and any animals who share that space, but also by the energies of everyone who has ever lived in that house or flat before them. And it's possible to sense all this when we walk into someone's home without knowing exactly what it is (see Exercise 24).

Exercise 24: How You (and Others) Feel about Your Home

Take a few moments to write down how you'd describe your home. Would you say it was:

- Elegant?
- Cosy?
- Makeshift?
- Comfortable?
- Welcoming?
- Untidy?
- Stark?
- Bohemian?
- Or what?

Have any friends, family or visitors commented upon how they feel about your home? If so, what have they said? Make a note of their comments.

Write down how you feel about your home. Do you love it? Hate it? Or is it just a place to live?

Everything in your home has an effect upon you, from the smallest object to the largest design feature. Every object you possess contains the emanations of the people who previously owned it, as well as the energy of the object's creator. The buildings we live and work in are made up of constantly changing energy, which, as we saw in the previous chapter, is made up of atoms and molecules through which the Chi or subtle energy of the Universe flows. And since you're energetically connected with everything in the Universe, you are therefore not separate from your home. Your home is alive and has consciousness—just the same as you!

Your home is a receptacle for your thoughts and feelings and therefore reflects your inner state. In a sense, it's an extension of your body. You may not be able to feel the energies moving around your home but believe me, they'll be influencing how you're feeling emotionally and may well be affecting your health.

In her book, *Sacred Space*, Denise Linn tells us that "...homes are nourished by how we hold them in our hearts." She goes on to say that our homes "...have a living spirit that is sustained through the reverence and the love we hold for them. Without that care they become inanimate and lifeless... Your home is an evolving creative being...(It) can be your ally or it can be an adversary...(it) interfaces with you and through that connection you can both grow...and evolve. The regard in which you hold your home can rouse an ancient and replenishing spirit from the deep to fill your home; this power can heal you in the very centre of your soul and heart."

The ancient Chinese art of Feng Shui (pronounced Fung Shway) is all about knowing precise techniques which can provide this nourishment and support for yourself within your home. Developed over 4000 years ago, it provides methods of changing and re-aligning the Chi flowing through your house or flat in order to create the most harmonious environment for you. Making the necessary adjustments to allow a free flow of this vital energy is seen to facilitate good fortune in life, career and relationships and also to enhance health and well-being. It also offers solutions or "cures" for changing unhelpful energies which may have been caused either by the orientation of the building, the discharge of your emotions (or those of previous owners) or obstructive energies caused by the wrong placement of objects and furniture. It's a very conscious way of changing our outer world to help re-balance the inner one.

The knowledge and practise of Feng Shui involves various elements such as mathematical calculations and Chinese Astrology. The practitioner also has to learn about Yin and Yang (these are mutually dependent but opposite types of Chi energy), and the Five Elements (these are different types of energy drawn from Nature—Fire, Earth, Metal, Water and Wood. In addition they must be able to interpret the Bagua (which is a template showing which areas of your home relate to various aspects of your life), and know how to use colour and placements to enhance the flow of Chi. Feng Shui also involves ways of refining the levels of Chi, which is known as Space Clearing, and this practise requires clearing clutter from the home beforehand.

Piles of clutter, even when hidden out of sight in cupboards and wardrobes, are a natural gathering space for negative energies. The more negative energy accumulates, the denser the atmosphere in your home will become. Side effects of this can be lack of energy, foggy thinking, general inertia or laziness, sadness and depression. It can affect your immune system and in some cases it can even contribute towards serious illness.

The effects of Space Clearing allow you to lift the vibrations of Chi in your home to the point where it isn't just a *home* but a dwelling that is a *sanctuary* as well. In other words, it enables your home to become a sacred space that nurtures and supports you through all the ups and downs of your life.

Every Feng Shui practitioner I've ever come across has agreed that trying to implement cures, placements and other techniques is rarely effective without having cleared the clutter out of our homes first! Regular Space Clearing is also recommended especially after illness, death or any traumatic event. It's also excellent for helping to clear the way towards making much needed changes in your life and attitude. And we could all do with some help with that from time to time!

You can learn the basics of doing each of these things on your own by following the guidelines I'm going to set out in this chapter and Chapter 10. Deeper guidance and insights into both techniques will be found in the writings of Denise Linn, Karen Kingston and others (see the Further Information and Suggested Reading section at the back of this book). Once you've cleared your clutter and learnt about the fundamental aspects of Space Clearing for yourself, you're then in a position to try implementing other Feng Shui techniques to enhance the energy of where you live.

Before we go any further with this subject, let me clarify what I mean when I talk about "clearing clutter". I don't mean that you have to suddenly become obsessively tidy! I'm not advocating that you live in a Zen minimalist environment devoid of ornamentation. Nor am I suggesting that you plump up all the cushions on the sofa just as soon as someone vacates it, or that you sweep away each and every speck of dust immediately when it catches your eye!

No. When you're in the middle of doing something, there's always going to be times when a number of things are lying around the place which are simply part of the task in which you've engaged. Think about what the kitchen is like when you're cooking. In the process, you may find yourself surrounded by a number of pots and pans, plus various utensils, dishes, condiments, herbs and spices in the cooking area. That's fine! It may look untidy for a while, but there's a purpose to it. Once the cooking is finished, you then wash up and put those things away where they belong. Think "tidy" in these terms. Not "tidy" meaning pristine, sterile, regimented and devoid of any spontaneity or creativity.

Clutter builds up when things never get put away, when there's too much stuff and not enough storage, or when piles of things end up strewn on the floor, under beds, chairs and sofas or stuffed into cupboards all higgledy-piggledy because they don't have a "home".

Clutter creates stuck energy, which in turn creates chaos in your life and makes you feel disorganised. Physical clutter in the home means mental clutter in the mind. It can make you tired and keep you emotionally bound up with the past. If you feel in a rut, there will be a corresponding stuckness in some part of your home. Clearing it not only clears your *outer* space but also your *inner* space as well. Getting rid of clutter will help you clear the way for new things, new people and new opportunities to come into your life.

Exercise 25 can help you begin the process of clearing out clutter and ultimately enhancing the Chi in your home.

Exercise 25: Preparation For Clutter-Clearing

The best way of starting this process is to take a cool, dispassionate look at the state of every room in your home, including the kitchen and bathroom. If the very idea of this makes you want to run a mile, *don't worry!* You can take it in stages and do it one room at a time.

On the other hand, if the exercise flags up no particular difficulties for you, you can make an overall assessment of each room fairly quickly and then set about seeing which one you want to tackle first.

Take a notebook and go to the first room and write down the name of it at the top of the page; e.g., "sitting room". All you have to do at this stage is to stand in the doorway and look into the room as calmly and objectively as you can and answer the following questions about it:

1. Can you move around the room easily without either bumping into furniture or having to step over things which are lying on the floor?

2. Is there so much clutter in certain parts that you can't actually access particular areas?

3. Are the furniture surfaces clear of everything except intended ornamentation or practical objects—telephones, phone books, ashtrays and lamps?

4. Can you use the furniture for the purpose it serves?

5. If you've got clutter, where are the worst areas? Make a note of the worst clutter zones with the worst areas at the top of the list.

Be honest with yourself when you're answering the questions. For example, if you have a desk which is covered with papers and books and all kinds of extraneous bits and pieces, and it's like that *permanently*, you can't answer "yes" to question 3! Likewise, if you have a dining table which is groaning under an assortment of objects, it isn't being used as a table for eating purposes!

If you have any cupboards and storage areas in the room, open the doors and drawers one by one and look inside. Then answer the following question:

6. Is the inside so packed and jumbled you can't tell what you've got in there?

When you've done this, you can move on to the next room and do the same thing, again answering questions 1 through to 6. Carry on with this process until you've assessed every room in your home.

If you feel overwhelmed or despondent about how much clutter is around, and you don't feel strong enough to do every room immediately, commit yourself to assessing another one or two rooms later in the day. Make yourself a promise that if you don't finish this exercise the first day, you'll continue with it the following day and keep going with this assessment each day until you've finished it. The important thing is to keep up a momentum. If you don't do this, you're in danger of losing impetus and finding it more difficult to start on the real task of clearing your clutter.

Most of us have areas of clutter which need to be cleared and if they're not obvious then they're hidden behind drawers and cupboard doors! Some people only have a bit of clutter, others have rather too much, and some of us are almost totally submerged in it!

Exercise 26 will help you to determine how all this clutter is affecting your life and your emotions.

Exercise 26: How Does This Clutter Make Me Feel?

Ask yourself the following questions and write the answers in your notebook:

1. In the areas where clutter collects, how do those places make you feel?

2. Is your clutter a minor, major or overwhelming problem?

3. If your clutter has got seriously out of hand, when did this start?

4. Was there some event in your life which triggered it?

Some people may find themselves getting very emotional when they think about these questions. If this is so for you, then before you even *start* trying to clear your clutter, please turn to Chapters 12 and 13 on EmoTrance and Emotional Freedom Technique (EFT). Here you'll find how to use simple techniques to dissolve and let go of these emotions. Any distress you may be feeling may be because of stuck emotional patterns which have blocked up the flow of your inner Chi. Once these have been released, (and you may be surprised at how quickly, easily and painlessly you can do this) you'll then be in a better place to let go of that inner clutter that is keeping you bogged down, and which is reflected in the outer clutter around your home.

If, on the other hand, you're OK about these questions and you've completed Exercise 25 (page 74), you're now ready to start on the clearing.

Before you begin acting on Exercise 26, bear in mind a few general rules:

- Decide how much time you're going to spend doing the clearing and set an alarm to go off when it's time to stop. This helps to break down the time into manageable chunks. Working this way can make a big difference in actually doing something about it instead of putting it off endlessly. Think what it would be like if your working day wasn't defined by a certain number of hours with time off for meal breaks. Yes, I know we all tend to go overtime, but there's always a point where we pack up and go home. Putting a time limit on this task (allow yourself at least 2 to 3 hours, especially if there's a lot to do) gives you the chance of making a reasonable dent in the work and helps makes a daunting job seem less overwhelming.

- Start by clearing the easiest room in your home. Many people choose to begin in the bathroom. This is a particularly good starting place for people with major clutter problems. By starting with the smallest room there will be less stuff to go through which means that quite quickly you'll be able to notice how much better you feel when it's cleared! Feeling that magical difference in your own energy and the energy of the room in question is grist to the mill and will give you impetus to continue working through the rest of your home.

- No matter how big or small the problem, only ever tackle *one* area at a time. This may entail just working on a small corner and slowly moving around the room tackling each clutter zone as you come to it.

- Golden rule of clutter clearing: If you don't *love* it or *use* it—*lose it!* People often keep things "just in case". When you do this you're programming your subconscious mind to prepare for a situation of neediness, and as a result, you may well find that such a situation arises. Many people hold on to things they've been given simply because of their associations with the person who gave the present. This is fine if you *like* the gift, but if you don't like it, every time you look at it or pick it up, you're linking into negative energy that then radiates out into your home.

- Always plan to get rid of your junk immediately. Don't have it hanging around. If you have a bag full of items ready for the charity shop, take them there that very day. Anything that has to be thrown away should be put into the bin immediately. This gives you very quick clearance. Notice how you feel when these objects are no longer in the house. Enjoy the increased clarity and flow in the vibrations of your home.

OK. Now, find three medium-sized boxes or big black bin liners (you'll need to have a stock of these boxes and/or bin bags) and keep them beside you as you go through things. Label them:

- Keep/Relocate/File
- Donate/Give Away/Bin
- Don't know

Just getting things sorted into three different piles is a quick and effective way of managing stuff as you encounter it. Whatever you decide to keep can be resorted and replaced when you've cleared out the junk. Anything you're not sure about can be put away and decided on later, ideally with the help of a trusted friend. However, if you're doing this on your own, Exercise 27 will give you a few good ways to check whether you need to keep or get rid of an object.

Exercise 27: Checking Out the "Don't Know" Items

If you're unsure of whether to keep or dispose of an item, stop what you're doing, close your eyes and come into your breath. Follow your breath for a few moments and centre yourself as best you can.

Now pick up the item and hold it in your hands.

Notice how your energy responds. Go with the first response you're aware of and don't try to be logical or analytic about it. If you have a sense of your energies sinking or fading, then this object needs to go because it's draining you on some level. Try to accept this and don't question why. *This object needs to go.*

If, on the other hand, your energies feel as though they're expanding or lifting, then you should keep it because it nourishes you energetically. Again, don't question it or try to analyse why.

If you don't feel anything, try asking yourself, "Why am I keeping this?"

Go inside and listen for the answer. It can come very quickly. Again, go with the first response that comes up and don't try to analyse it!

If this still doesn't bring clarity, then a sure-fire way to find out whether you need to keep this article or not is to put it away in a box and leave it in a place where you can forget about it. Three months later, dig it out and look at it again. Trust me—*if you haven't missed it, you don't need it—get rid of it!*

Sentimental clutter is often the hardest to let go. For example, keeping old letters from ex-lovers means that at some level you still haven't come to terms with the ending of that relationship. If you encounter real difficulties with sentimental stuff, you may need to use EFT or EmoTrance to clear your blocks to letting go of these things. If necessary, don't be afraid to seek the help of a practitioner. Details on how to find practitioners can be found at in the Further Information and Suggested Reading at the back of the book.

When the timer goes off, put your boxes to one side until the next session (hopefully the very next day!). Clean up and do something else like putting stuff you've decided to throw out in the dustbin, or taking your cast-offs to the charity shop.

A few words about paperwork: with more and more of us working from home, paperwork can accumulate quickly and become a real energy drain. It's very easy to make a clearance only to let it pile up again. This is something you need to tackle *regularly!* Once you've cleared it, commit yourself to keeping an eye on any signs of it mounting up again. Don't let it get out of hand. Remind yourself about what it's doing to your personal energy and the energy in your home. The more it piles up, the more it drains your energy and blocks the Chi. The longer you leave it, the more daunting and insurmountable it may become. You'll feel so much better once you've dealt with it.

Additional pointers:

- Get rid of objects you associate with sadness, negativity or illness.
- Chuck out old magazines and newspapers.
- Go through your medicine cupboard and get rid of bottles of out-of-date pills and potions.
- Discard food in kitchen cupboards and the fridge that is past its shelf life.
- Throw away old makeup, bath or beauty preparations.
- Get rid of odd socks and tidy up the drawer where you keep them. Denise Linn swears this can have a major beneficial effect on depression!
- Get rid of anything you haven't worn in 2 to 3 years no matter how good it is and especially if it's too big or too small.
- Weed out any bad clothes or shoe buys you've made (and make a vow *never* to go comfort-shopping when you're feeling low or

depressed).

- Clear out the clutter in handbags and trouser pockets.
- Get broken things mended or get rid of them.

You could also benefit from clearing out the clutter in the car! And don't forget the boot!

Spring is a particularly good time to tackle clutter—though any time is a good time!

The old tradition of Spring Cleaning is based on the understanding of Spring being a time of renewal, so it's good to clean and mend things, polish the furniture, get rid of junk and fling open all the windows to let in clean fresh air after the stuffiness of Winter. By the way, the simple act of cleaning your windows can have an effect on the clarity in your life. Try it and see!

When we keep putting things off, they hang over us. The very thought of them causes pressure and brings us down. Leaving things undone is bad for your energy, so have a look at your procrastination levels! Do those tasks which need doing.

Don't keep unwanted gifts simply because you're afraid that the people who gave them to you might visit your home and notice they're missing. Nine times out of ten they don't notice—or if they do, they don't comment—but if it happens, you could always say it got broken or something. Aim to surround yourself only with the things that you use and the things that you *love*.

Always clear junk away from the entrance to your home. Hats and coats hanging from pegs or a jumble of shoes, boots or trainers on the floor, make obstacles to the energy flow of your environment. Keep these things in a cupboard. Your front door is like the mouth of your home. This is where the Chi enters. It *must* have clear passage otherwise it's going to get blocked from the word go. Likewise, if you have a hall table, beware letting it become a repository for junk mail, old newspapers, shopping bags or the like. Plants are really nice things to have in your entrance hall if you have the space, but make sure they have enough light and that they won't suffer from being in a draught where they are. Also, make sure they're healthy. Dead or dying plants in this area make for a very depressing energy to greet you as soon as you come in the door.

And finally, to complete all the clearing you've done, why not consider clearing out your colon and look into some cleansing programmes? Believe me, a thorough inner cleanse can work wonders on your sense of well-being and your energy levels!

To work out whether you need to do this, Karen Kingston suggests you eat a small handful of sunflower seeds and wait to see how long it is before they emerge from your other end! If they appear in your stools within 10 to 12 hours your colon is in pretty good condition. If it takes longer (and some people have to wait for several days before the seeds reappear) then you should definitely investigate a herbal colon cleanse or some colonic irrigation to clean out your system. You'll feel *wonderful* after you've done this! It's a very physical way of clearing clutter on an inner level.

After all this, you'll have released so much stuck energy in your body and your home, you'll feel light as a feather!

Chapter 10

Space Clearing and Creating a Sacred Space

Stagnant Chi can build up in our homes in several ways. As we've already seen, it can be caused by the accumulation of clutter. It's also constantly amassing from any negative vibrations spilling out of people who currently inhabit the dwelling. In addition, it's caused by the residual emotional energies of previous occupants of the home. It's not helped by emanations from nearby mobile phone masts, or indeed any other electromagnetic pollution from equipment such as televisions, computers and microwaves.

As you can see, there's an endless flow of this junk that causes negative energy and psychic debris to ripple out and build up in the very fabric of buildings. It accumulates in the walls and corners of rooms, in all the hidden nooks and crannies, and any place where the walls of the home meet the ceilings. In her book *Creating Sacred Space with Feng Shui*, Karen Kingston calls this "psychic gunge"! It's a very good description of what is basically stuck energy that needs to be unblocked, and allowed to flow. So if you really want to have the Chi flowing through your home in a way that enhances your environment and creates a sanctuary in which to live, you need to do some Space Clearing, which in and of itself will help to make your home into a sanctuary.

Exactly what *is* Space Clearing? Karen Kingston describes it as, "…the art of cleansing and consecrating spaces." It's about performing a ritual, that is a synthesis of some native rituals for clearing energy, and Feng Shui principles that can be used to lift the Chi to the highest levels in your home. It's not difficult to do. And all it requires is some time, commitment and intention.

You can use Space Clearing on an occasional basis as a part of your spring cleaning, after some very vigorous clutter clearing, or more regularly to maintain a good flow of energy in your home. Bear in mind that the nature of Chi is to be forever changing, so there'll be a number of times in your life when Space Clearing can be very helpful, such as:

- selling your home (it can help attract buyers),
- moving into a new home or office (clears the energies of previous occupants),
- after sickness in the home or after an accident,

- if you want to make a fresh start and take a new direction in your life,
- after the death in the home of a person or an animal,
- after big life changes like marriage, divorce or the birth of a child,
- if you're feeling stuck in your life, your job or in a dead-end relationship,
- if you've had difficult visitors or guests in your space,
- if you're feeling tired or drained all the time, or
- if you've been burgled.

It also enhances the placements recommended by Feng Shui and helps you to manifest what you want in your life. In addition, it also aids your spiritual development, increases your vitality, changes atmospheres and can even improve your sex life!

So how do we begin?

Well, if you've cleared out your clutter then you've already begun! Clearing clutter is *absolutely essential* to doing any Space Clearing. So don't even think about Space Clearing until you've dealt with your clutter.

The whole process of Space Clearing requires some advance planning as there are various things you need to arrange, prepare or acquire before you start:

- Make sure you have the permission of anyone else in your home to perform this ritual. This doesn't mean that they have to be present when you perform it, or that they have to help you with it
- When you do the ritual, it's important not to have anyone else around in your home unless you've already agreed to be working with a friend or partner on the ritual. This means, if you have children you need to have arranged for them to be looked after by someone else all day. You also need to ensure that your partner or anyone else sharing your home will be out all day as well. Don't worry about pets being around. Animals usually love Space Clearing and are very happy about the changes in energy that occur
- Don't do any Space Clearing if you're ill, run down, or tired
- Karen Kingston recommends that women shouldn't space clear during either their monthly periods or when pregnant. This is because the female energies are directed inwards during menstruation towards cleansing and preparing for possible conception. And in pregnancy, the focus is on maintaining a pure space within to carry

the child. By directing your energies outwards into an activity like Space Clearing at these times, you're going against your natural state of being which is to direct your focus *inside* your body

In order to do the Space Clearing, you'll also need to acquire several "props" (if you haven't already got them) as follows:

Joss Sticks and Holders: These are widely available in a variety of Indian hardware shops, health food retailers and other stores. Choose Joss Sticks which have an aroma that you like. Some of them have a very sweet perfume which isn't to everyone's taste. Take time to find the right aroma for you, because using one you don't like in the Space Clearing isn't helpful either to your energies or the energies of your home. (Remember how in the previous chapter, I told you the importance of having things in your home which you like or, preferably, *love*.)

Incense Burners, Charcoal and Incense: Incense burners are available in most Indian shops that sell devotional objects. You'll need to buy packs of little round pieces of charcoal used especially for burning incense. You'll also need to buy a pack of incense granules. Again take time to choose ones with an aroma that you really like. My personal preference for these granules are the ones made by the monks of Prinknash Abbey—I like the one called Basilica—but there are plenty of others to choose from. Both the charcoal rounds and the incense can be bought from specialist shops and outlets (see Further Information and Suggested Reading at the back of the book).

Bells: Ideally, you'll need two bells—one larger and one smaller (these are the traditional sort that you ring by waving the bell back and forth so the clapper sounds the bell). Larger bells with deeper sounds are good for breaking up stagnant energy. Smaller, tinkly bells are wonderful for using after the big bells, as they help to refine and call in the higher levels of Chi. Choosing bells is a very individual matter. It's really important to choose bells that feel right for you. Denise Linn says that, "...a bell that you love and honour will clear your home faster than the most pristine, valuable bell in the world." Try to find a bell made with copper in it if you can, as these are excellent for energy work. Copper is a wonderful conductor of energy and the combination of the copper and the vibrations of the bell form a purifying energy harmonic.

You don't have to go mad and spend huge amounts of money on your bells. You might even be able to borrow one or both of them if you don't want to go to the expense of buying them. Finding two bells with contrasting tones (one deeper and one higher) that you find pleasing is all you need to begin with. Later, if you want to get into Space Clearing more deeply, you may decide that you want to acquire more specialist bells like Balinese Temple bells or silver bells. You might at some point like to become the owner of a

Singing Bowl. These are bowl-shaped bells which send out a spiral sound in ever widening circles. They enable energy to be invoked and cleared at the same time and are therefore particularly helpful in space clearing.

A Rattle: These come in many shapes and sizes and are good for soothing and smoothing the energy of a home. (Think of how small rattles are frequently given to babies to help them feel calm and safe.) If you can't afford a rattle, then buy one of those big household boxes of matches, tip out half the contents and rattle the half empty box as a substitute. It works! You can experiment with how many matches you need to leave inside to get the sound you want.

A Drum: It is possible to do Space Clearing without a drum, but if you decide to get one for this purpose, you'll be very glad that you did. Drums are really good for breaking up dense and congested energy; e.g., the residue from heavy emotions like anger, sadness or grief, or if there's been death or sickness in the house. As you drum around your home, the sounds and vibrations you make are going to clear *your* energies as well! Traditionally, the drum most used for Space Clearing is the round, hand-held Native American drum. You could, in fact, use any kind of drum as long as it's made from animal skin and wood. (Animal skins provide the best sound for use in space clearing. However, if you are averse to using items made from animals, then you would have to use an alternative kind of drum and base your choice on finding something that provides the most deeply reverberant sound.) The choice of drum is entirely up to you, and it doesn't have to be big or expensive. If you can't find a drum to suit your taste and pocket, then don't worry. Leave out the drumming part of the ritual I'm going to describe and just use the bells and the rattle.

All of the above items should be honoured by being kept in a special place.

Once you've cleared your clutter and collected all the items you'll need for the ritual, then you should set a date for doing the Space Clearing. New and Full Moon days are recommended, but not essential. Sometimes the simple necessity of needing to do the ritual in the first place makes any day the right day!

The night before you perform the ritual, there are three things you can do: 1) spend time deciding what your intentions are for doing this ceremony, and write them down, 2) create a special altar to act as a focal point during the ritual, and 3) invoke the spirit or angel of your home to help you prepare for and perform the Space Clearing.

The following exercises look at each of these things one by one.

Exercise 28: Writing Out Your Intention

The night before the Space Clearing, spend some time thinking about what you'd like the ritual to help you manifest. Get a notebook and pen and jot down all the things you'd like to achieve from doing this. Then look at what you've written and choose the one, or ones, that feel most important.

Now take a clean piece of paper and write out your intention clearly and simply. Don't write anything lengthy, just a short paragraph or sentence will do. Start by writing: "My intention is_____" and then go on to describe it.

Here's some suggestions:

- To clear all the energies from my home which prevent me from moving forward in my life.
- To remove all the obstacles to my business flourishing and to money flowing into my life.
- To let go of all the residues of my sadness/negativity/depression so I may create a home full of positive energy.
- To create a home full of light and positive healthy energy which will support and nourish all of us who live here in all of our endeavours.
- To facilitate an ever-expanding spiritual consciousness on all levels of my being.

You can of course write down more than one thing, if you wish.

After you've finished writing, sign your name, and place the piece of paper in a clean envelope and seal it.

When you're ready to do the invocation, place this envelope on the altar to declare your intention before you invoke your House Spirit or Angel. Leave it on the altar throughout the whole Space Clearing. When the Space Clearing is finished, burn it without opening it. Burning is a good way of sending things to a higher level. (*Please make sure you burn the envelope safely*—hold it over a sink and have a metal or ceramic bowl to drop it into when you can no longer hold it).

If you'd like to create an altar, this is what you do.

Exercise 29: Creating an Altar

The best place for your altar is in the main room of your home (usually the sitting room). A small table or chest is ideal to use as the base (make sure it's dusted and clean). If you don't have anything suitable, then a mantel shelf will do. Or improvise by using a strong cardboard box of the right size, but make sure it's sturdy and has a flat surface that can bear the weight of candles, vases and holders, etc. The main thing is to ensure that the altar is raised up off the ground. Set up your altar in a place which won't get in the way of your Space Clearing. You need to be able to leave it in place for the duration, as it forms a focal point of the ritual.

Spread a nice clean cloth or piece of fabric over the surface of your altar. Most people like to put a vase of fresh flowers there. You could also set up some candlesticks with candles or arrange some tea lights in little votive jars. Alternatively, if you have a wide shallow dish, fill it with water, and put in some floating candles. Cutting off some flower heads and placing them in amongst the floating candles makes a very attractive offering. You could also place a favourite crystal on the altar (make sure crystals are clean by washing them under running water beforehand and placing them out to dry in the sunshine), or special pebbles, shells or feathers, etc., which you love. Put out your joss sticks and holder, your incense burner plus charcoal and incense. Don't forget to have some matches ready and a little saucer for spent matches. Finally, place your drum, bells and rattle beside the altar ready for when you need them.

Make your altar a pleasing sight and don't crowd it with too many objects.

You might like to invoke the spirit or angel of your home (in other words, your House Guardian—yes there's one in every home!—to be with you when you do the clearing), because it's always good to have some help in these matters! You don't have to know the name of your house guardian or even what it looks like. It's enough to believe that there's a benevolent energy watching over and guarding your space. If you don't believe in such things, then don't worry—you don't have to do this bit if you don't want to (Exercise 30).

Exercise 30: Invoking the Guardian of Your Home

When you're ready to do the ritual, make sure you have the room to yourself. Put the phone on answer and tell anyone else in the house that you don't want to be interrupted.

You're going to invoke your Guardian with the lighting of a special candle or tea light which is separate from the others you may have set out on your altar. See if you can find a particularly nice votive jar in which to place it. Make sure the container is clean and that you've got a new tea light ready to use.

Turn off all the electric lights. Put on some music that you find gentle, uplifting and meditative. Light all the candles—except for the special one reserved for your house guardian—and light the joss sticks.

As the joss sticks start to fill the room with their aroma, spend a bit of time meditating. Sit with your envelope of intentions in your lap and start following your breath (Exercise 14, page 44). Sit quietly, concentrating on your breathing and letting the thoughts pass through you like clouds moving across the sky. Carry on with this for about 10 minutes, slowly bringing your mind to focus upon the fact that you are going to invoke your House Guardian to help you tomorrow in cleansing your space and creating a sacred space for yourself.

When you're ready, move towards your altar and place your "intention envelope" there. Reach for the matches to light your special candle. As you do this, make a silent affirmation that you're lighting this candle for the Guardian spirit or angel of your home.

Once the candle is lit, place your hands in the prayer position and solemnly and reverently address your House Guardian. Begin with the words: "Dear Guardian of my Home, please bless me with your presence." Ask it to infuse your whole being when you're sleeping to help you become an energy channel for the highest levels of Chi during the Space Clearing the following day.

Thank the Guardian for protecting and watching over your home. Ask it to help you with the work you're going to do tomorrow, and to support you in carrying out your intentions afterwards. Ask that it give its benevolent blessings to this work and please to continue to guard and watch over all who live in the home with you. You can add in anything else which you feel is appropriate.

End by thanking the Guardian in advance for its help and complete the invocation with "So Be It" or "Amen" (which means the same thing).

Afterwards, return to your meditation and continue with this until it feels time to stop. Then put out the joss sticks, extinguish the candles and go to bed.

There are many different ways of Space Clearing, but I'm going to explain a method I've compiled from various techniques and always found to be effective. Purists might tell you that I've missed out certain things, but this way is simple and easy enough to get you started and allow you to experience the wonders of changing the atmosphere in your home. The most important thing in Space Clearing is your intention. If you hold your intention (i.e., the desired outcome of the ritual) in your mind throughout the whole procedure, you will always make the changes you want to make. For other techniques and to explore this whole subject more deeply, I highly recommend that you read the Denise Linn and Karen Kingston books listed in the Further Information and Suggested Reading section at the back of this book.

Please don't be put off by the length of the following explanations. It actually takes longer to give you written explanations than it would be to show you what to do! However, because I can't physically be with you when you do your Space Clearing, the least I can do is to make sure that I've explained it all as clearly as possible.

The best way to do Space Clearing is to do one room after another, so you work through your entire living space in one go. Much of course depends on how big your home is. If you live in a large house, you may need to enlist the help of a friend, relative or partner who's willing to work with you, so you can get the whole thing done in one day. However, this requires that you both work out exactly who is going to do what beforehand. For the average two-bedroom home, however, it's usually pretty easy to do it all at once and on your own. The actual Space Clearing ritual can be done in under an hour for the average sized home.

The day after the invocation, you need to get up bright and early as you will be devoting the whole day to this. Do a 15- to 20-minute meditation and connect back to your House Guardian. Ask again for guidance and assistance in the work you are going to do.

Your first task is to clean everywhere in your home very thoroughly including the kitchen and bathroom and any separate room with a toilet. Uh-oh! I can hear shuddering and groaning at the very idea of this as I write! Bear with me! This is *not* a housekeeping manual you're reading. There are deeper and more profound meanings to all of this which can help to change your mood, health and energy levels. If you keep this in mind when you're giving your home a really good clean, you'll find this whole exercise tremendously gratifying. And if you're naturally tuned into energy, you'll also notice how the quality of the space you're cleaning becomes clearer and more refined as you work!

So, dust all the furniture, vacuum all the carpets and remember to clean underneath any furniture as a lot of dust, debris and stagnant Chi can collect there. Wash wooden floors with an appropriate cleaning fluid, and vacuum over all the upholstery of chairs and sofas with the upholstery attachment (if you have one). Remember to go over cushions and bedcovers as well and also to vacuum down the curtains in each room.

Put the fine nozzle on the vacuum cleaner and go round all the skirting boards and their ledges to get rid of any dust. Then turn the nozzle up towards the ceiling and sweep it around all the edges where the walls meet the ceilings. Make downward sweeps with the nozzle in all the corners of each room from the ceiling to the floor. Doing this not only removes any of the fine cobwebs that accumulate in corners but literally sucks out negative energy.

However, if you haven't got a vacuum with this kind of attachment, then you need to use the sound your hand makes when clapping instead to clear the stagnant energy. Exercise 31 describes how to do it.

Exercise 31: Clapping Down the Walls

Start by facing the front door of your home and go to the first corner either to the left or right of where you're standing. Start clapping with your hands above your head and clap loudly in the first corner all the way down from the ceiling to the floor. Do this several times while holding the intention that the area you're clapping is becoming totally clear of any stagnant energy.

At first, the sound you make with your clapping may have a slightly dull tone to it, but as you clap down the area a few times, you'll find the tone changes and that the sound becomes much crisper and clearer. When this happens, move on to the next corner.

Continue working down the corners of each and every room—*always working in a clockwise direction*—until you arrive back to where you first started.

About halfway through going round your home, you should find what Karen Kingston calls an "after twang" to your clapping (a sort of echo to each clap). This is when the clapping really begins to reverberate. When this happens it means you've started to clear that "psychic gunge" which was hanging around the corners of your home.

Make sure you wash your hands very thoroughly under running water after you've finished doing the clapping as this rinses away any psychic debris that may have become attracted to your aura during the process.

When you've finished all the cleaning and clapping, it's time to shift gears. Have a nice leisurely bath or shower and wash your hair. You could throw a couple of handfuls of rock salt into the bath water if you like, as this is especially helpful in clearing your aura of any bits of static energy which have become attached during all the work you've been doing. Put on some clean clothes. By feeling fresh and clean yourself, you'll be better able to sense when the atmosphere in your home has cleared.

For the next and final part of the Space Clearing, don't wear a watch or any jewellery. (Metals and stones attract energy and when you're clearing out negative stuff you don't want it accumulating in your jewellery!) Also take off any metal-framed glasses, remove coins from any pockets and *work barefoot* so you can sense the energies better and be more grounded. Put the phone on answer. Don't play any music. Have the place to yourself unless you've previously arranged to do this with a friend or a partner (in which case you need to have worked out beforehand who's going to do what at any given time). Don't drink any alcohol, but do drink plenty of pure spring water because you could get thirsty and it helps with the general cleansing process.

To prepare, begin by taking one of the little charcoal rounds and lighting it. Hold one edge of the round and put the lighted match to the other side of the round. When it ignites the charcoal, it fizzes and spits gently. Hold it between your fingers for a few seconds to make sure it's definitely been ignited. Sometimes it fizzes a bit and then stops, in which case you have to light it again. Once you're sure it's fizzing and burning through the charcoal, place it in the incense burner.

These little charcoal rounds get very hot and so does the incense burner, so it's therefore a good idea to have a small heat resistant tray or saucer on which to place the burner because you're going to be carrying it around with you from room to room later. You don't want to burn your fingers!

Place the incense burner on the altar you created the night before. Don't put the incense granules on immediately once you've lit the charcoal. If you try to do this when the charcoal is red hot, you'll just incinerate the incense and cause an unpleasant smell instead of simply heating it through to release its beautiful aroma. So, wait until the charcoal has become a grey, ash colour and has cooled down a bit. Then you can put some granules of incense on to release the aroma. I usually start the charcoal lighting part of this ritual just before I get into my bath after all the housework has been done. I find that by the time I've finished bathing, and washed and dried my hair, the charcoal has reached the right temperature for burning the incense.

Before you begin your Space Clearing, you need to practice Hara Breathing (Exercise 32), after which you're ready to start doing the Space Clearing.

Exercise 32: Hara Breathing

Stand in what you feel is the centre of your home, or at least, as close to the centre of the space as possible. Place your feet about shoulder's width apart and direct your attention down into your Hara, which is located the width of two finger below your navel (see Exercise 20, page 64).

Begin watching your breath by imagining you're breathing in and out through this place in your belly. This is your energetic centre and by focusing here you're centring and grounding yourself very strongly. Focus on the experience of being in your *body* rather than in your *head*. Do this for several minutes and be aware of your feet taking the weight of your body and your connection to the earth. Try to keep this connection all the way through the Space Clearing.

Then bring your intention for the Space Clearing firmly into focus and hold onto it throughout the whole of the following procedure.

Space Clearing and Creating Sacred Space

First Round of Clearing

Go into your "altar room" and very reverently take up your drum (if you've got one). If you haven't got one, then start your Space Clearing ritual from "Second Round of Clearing".

Bless your drum and thank it for what it's going to do for you. Hold it closely to you and imagine that it's a part of you. Run your hand lovingly around its rim.

Holding the drum, stand outside the main entrance or front door of your home and face the door. You're going to drum in a clockwise circle around the door. Imagine it's a clock face and sound the drum once at 9 o'clock, once at 12 o'clock, once at 3 o'clock and once at 6 o'clock. Go round the door doing this three more times. Then open the door and step into your home.

If for some reason you're unable (or unwilling!) to stand outside the main entrance and do this, then stand inside your home with your back to the front door and do the drumming as described above.

As you work with your drum, allow your wrist to be loose and relaxed and use your hand rather than your arm to do the drumming, otherwise you may get very tired. Let yourself be guided in terms of what rhythm you choose. If you're unsure, a heartbeat rhythm is always a good one to start with—da-dum, da-dum, da-dum. Use your intuition about the beats to use. Let the drum guide you. You may feel occasionally as though the drum is drumming you! Remember your Hara breathing throughout and just relax into this. Your breathing may deepen as you go round your home.

Now move towards the nearest corner of the space you're in. Hold your drum near the floor and drum up the corner towards the ceiling. *(Yes, up and not down the corner this time.)* Like the clapping, if the sound is dull, do it again until it's crisp and vibrant, which shows the energy is clear. (You're now refining the work you've done previously). When the drum sounds clear in the corner, move to the next one, sounding the drum as you move along the walls. When you get to the next corner, do the same thing. Keep going until you're back to where you began.

Finish off by standing in the centre of the room and moving the drum in a clockwise circle, sound it in each of the four directions—to the right side, towards the floor, to the left side and towards the ceiling.

Move on to the next room and do the same thing. Keep repeating this procedure in every room including the kitchen, bathroom and any rooms with separate toilets.

If your home is on several floors, start at the lowest level and work upwards around each floor until you reach the top of the house.

When you've done all the rooms like this, take the drum back to the "altar room". Thank it for the work it's done and place it carefully down beside the altar. You may find you need to add some more incense to the charcoal burner while you're there.

*If you've used a drum, simply move into the Second Round of Clearing and follow the directions below. However, if you haven't used a drum, your Space Clearing ritual will have to start with the big bell in place of the drum. In that case, start by reverently picking up the big bell and connecting with it as described for the drum. Take the bell **and the incense burner** to your front door. Leave the incense burner somewhere safe inside as you do the front door ritual. Stand outside the front door (if possible) and ring the bell at the 9 o'clock, 12 o'clock, 3 o'clock and 6 o'clock positions. Do this three* *more times as described for the drum in the First Round of Clearing. Then, when you step inside your home, pick up the incense burner and proceed from Ringing the Big Bell (see below):*

Second Round of Clearing

If you have used the drum for the First Round of Clearing, now pick up the bigger bell. Greet it with reverence, expand your consciousness into it and run your hand around its rim. Then, pick up the incense burner and head for the front door carrying both the bell and the incense burner.

Ringing the Big Bell

You're going to be carrying the incense in your left hand and ringing the bell with your right hand. You're going to waft the incense up towards the corners as you ring your bell, moving both from floor to ceiling. It sounds complicated, but you'll get the hang of it quite easily. Waft and ring up the first corner. If the bell sounds dull anywhere, keep ringing it until it becomes clear. Ring the bell and waft the incense as you walk along the wall to the next corner and do the same thing. Don't forget to include any small rooms with separate toilets. Go clockwise round each room, ringing the bell and wafting the incense into the corners from floor to ceiling until you get back to where you began. Finish your work in each room by putting down the incense burner and sounding the bell in each of the four directions—to the right side, towards the floor, to the left side and towards the ceiling. When you've finished, replace the incense burner on the altar, thank your bell, and put it down beside the altar. You may find you have to replenish the incense on the burner between rooms if it's burning quickly.

When you use the drum, or the drum followed by the big bell and incense, or just the big bell with the incense, you are clearing the energies. When you use the little bell—as per the next section—you're invoking the highest energies to fill your space.

Third Round of Clearing

Now pick up the smaller bell, greet it, and run your fingers around its rim. All you're going to do this time is to move around your home in a clockwise direction, ringing the bell in all the corners (but *not* up the corners) and along all the walls. By this time, the energies should really be very clear, but listen carefully and if the bell sounds a bit flat in certain places, keep ringing it until the sound is clear. Remember your aim now is to invoke high, pure energy. Finish off each room by ringing it in the four directions. Then, thank your bell and put it with the other instruments beside the altar. You could add one last sprinkling of incense to the charcoal now.

Smoothing the Energy and Sealing It In

Finally, pick up the rattle. You're going to use this to soothe and smooth all the energy in every room. Follow through the same process of greeting it— yes, even if it's just a humble household matchbox! Go straight to the nearest corner of the room, and shake the rattle in woodpecker-type movements. Again, as with the little bell, you don't need to work up the corners. All you need to do is to rattle it *towards* all the corners a few times. Move along the walls rattling fast and, moving in a clockwise direction, go to the next corner and so on till the room is complete.

Now you're going to seal the refined energies into the room. You don't have to rattle in the four directions. Just go to the door of the room and rattle in a straight line *down* the centre of the door from ceiling to floor. Imagine you're zipping it closed and sealing the entrance. Do this in all the rooms after you've rattled the corners and walls, moving clockwise around the home until you've completed the process. End by thanking your rattle and placing it beside the altar.

Complete the ritual by meditating for about 20 minutes in the "altar room". A few more pointers:

- The best time to do this is at the new or full moon, or at the beginning of spring. Alternatively, do it when prompted by any of the events or situations listed at the beginning of the chapter, or through other appropriate circumstances.

- If you live in a house, then it's good if you can do the Space Clearing with someone else as you can complete the whole process much quicker. You could each work simultaneously on separate floors to complete the general cleaning.

- If you're doing a house on your own, then, depending on its size, you may need to do the general cleaning on one day and the Space Clearing the day after. But if it's possible, try to do the house cleaning and the Space Clearing all on the same day.

- Don't try to clear anyone else's home. Leave this to the professionals (see the Further Information and Suggested Reading section at back of book).

Space Clearing Maintenance

Having gone to all the trouble of raising the vibration of Chi in your home, you'll almost certainly want to do everything you can to maintain it! The main thing is to make a commitment to not let clutter build up and get out of hand, and to keep on top of the housework! You'll have to re-do the Space

Clearing from time to time, and your increasing sensitivity to energy will help you to know when this needs to be done.

For simple maintenance between Space Clearings, try some of the ready-made bottles of Space Clearing Mists which contain a mixture of water laced with Flower Essences. You can buy them from most good health food shops. Squirt some around a room after any emotional disturbance or other energetic disruption.

Alternatively, you could make up your own. Buy a mister bottle (there are plenty of cheap ones around in garden centres for misting plants). Put a small amount of spring water in the bottom and add a few drops of flower essence to make the mixture. Here are some suggestions:

- For any release of negative energy, add two drops Crab Apple.
- For creating tranquillity after an argument, add two drops Lavender.
- After an accident, add two drops Rescue Remedy.

Instead of misting Flower Essences, you can also throw pinches of rock salt into all the corners of the room where the disturbance happened.

Every morning when you get up, make a ritual of lighting a votive candle to your House Guardian to honour it and ask for its daily protection and blessings. Make sure the votive candle is in a fireproof container and set upon a small mat to protect the base from getting too hot and damaging the surface where it's situated. Make sure it's in a safe place where it's not going to be knocked over by children or animals. If you are *absolutely satisfied* that it's safe to do so, then leave the flame burning all day. Extinguish it if you're going out and re-light it on your return.

Some good old fashioned house cleaning will always do an amazing job at perking up the energies in your home!

You can use music to lift the vibrations of Chi. For a quick fix remedy for congested energy, play some African drum music. Flute music will have a wonderful cleansing effect on the Chi, as will the sound of singing bowls (see the Further Information and Suggested Reading section at back of book).

Keep your home cleansed and perfumed by using joss sticks or an aroma burner on a regular basis.

If you've learnt the second degree of Reiki, drawing the first symbol up in the corners of each room is very cleansing and also brings the wonderful healing energy of Reiki into your home.

Therapists of any sort should clear the energies of their therapy rooms regularly. If you work from home, it's not a good idea to sleep in the same room where you regularly see clients.

Devoting time to purifying and raising the levels of Chi in your home can be an empowering and uplifting experience for you. You'll notice a lightness and clarity in your environment afterwards, which instantly makes you feel better. Enjoy knowing that you can make such a difference on both an inner and outer level by doing this, and take pleasure in seeing your life becoming more meaningful and expansive.

Chapter 11
Energy Medicine

Everything we think, feel and see is going to have an effect on the body–mind, which in turn affects our emotions. And anything that affects body–mind–emotions is going to have an effect on the energy body (which is a kind of reflection of the physical body).

The energy body is made up of several inter-related energy systems. Of these, the most widely known ones are (1) the Meridians (the pathways through which the subtle energy flows), (2) the Aura, (the multi-layered energy sheath surrounding the physical body), and (3) the Chakras (the energy centres which spin and draw in Chi from the Universe and distribute it through the meridians).

The quality of Chi flowing through all our energy systems fluctuates from day to day, depending on what's happening in our lives. As I said in Chapter 10, difficult or traumatic experiences cause disturbances creating a kind of inner "psychic gunge" or blocked Chi. Whenever and wherever this happens, it will cause a knock-on effect in the rest of the energy system. Prolonged blocks and disturbances can eventually damage our mental, emotional and physical health, and can also affect us on a spiritual level as well.

Unfortunately, because we're all human, we all get blocked from time to time! So every now and again we go into a wobble and sometimes the wobble can feel like an earthquake! That's part of the human condition. But, it is possible to address some of the effects of these disturbances by doing a kind of inner Feng Shui that supports general health and well-being and also helps us to deal with emotional pain.

So, how do we do that?

Well, you've actually already started if you've been trying out the techniques and practises I've been giving you in this book. However, in addition to the many holistic self-help techniques you've learnt so far, there are other, more specific techniques you can employ. The first one I want to tell you about can be used to target the smooth running of the meridians. This can be achieved very simply through the use of an exercise derived from the field of Energy Medicine.

What Is Energy Medicine?

Energy Medicine is a generic term used to describe energy-based therapies which are grounded in the principle that the body, mind and spirit are essentially interconnected. Donna Eden, an internationally recognised pioneer in this particular field, describes it as "...the science and art of optimizing your energies to help your body and mind function at their best". She goes on to say that, "Energy is the living, vibrating ground of your being, and it is your body's natural self-healing elixir, its natural medicine. This medicine, this *energy* medicine, feeds body and soul, and...restores your natural vitality."*

Energy Medicine involves the sending, receiving or moving of energy through all the energy systems. The term *Energy Medicine* therefore covers a wide range of techniques like Acupuncture, Acupressure, Applied Kinesiology, Endorphin Techniques, Polarity Therapy, Reiki, Reflexology, Shiatsu, and Therapeutic Touch, etc. Magnets, crystals and aromas are sometimes used, as well as movements, postures and hands-on techniques. Exercises like Qi Gong, Tai Chi and Yoga also help to move energy, as do visualisations (including guided meditations), endorphin techniques and EmoTrance.

An Energy Medicine practitioner may also use massage, tapping, and other forms of touch to connect energy centres or points, or trace energy pathways to promote healing. In this way, the practitioner works with the body's connective tissue that acts as a kind of electrical semi-conductor, thereby bringing about the re-balancing and restoration of energy flow. Energy Medicine techniques facilitate an increase in vitality and well-being, strengthen the immune system, and also serve to clear and balance emotional blocks caused by disruptions in the energy system.

Blocked or suppressed emotions cause the meridian channels to clog up and affect our health. The meridians are like inner rivers and the Chi they transport has a dynamic effect on every vital organ and system in the human body including your cells, moods and thoughts.

There are 12 major meridians running through the subtle anatomy and each one is named after either an organ or a function. These are the:

- Stomach
- Spleen
- Heart (considered to be the "Emperor" of the meridians)
- Small Intestine

---

* From *Energy Medicine for Women* by Donna Eden with David Feinstein.

Finding the River

- Bladder
- Kidney
- Pericardium—also known as Circulation–Sex. (The Pericardium is a fluid-filled sac that surrounds and protects the heart. The meridian of Circulation–Sex contributes towards this heart protection and also governs the hormones and circulation)
- Triple Warmer (a large meridian linked to our immune system and very much connected to our flight-or-fight-response)
- Gallbladder
- Liver
- Lung, and
- Large Intestine

In addition, there's the Central Meridian, which helps keep your Central Nervous System working, and the Governing Meridian, which helps pump a fluid known as cerebrospinal fluid around the Central Nervous system, delivering nutrients and removing wastes and toxins. These two meridians are linked with each other.

One of the easiest ways of keeping your energies humming is to trace the channels of your meridians with your hands to encourage the energy to flow freely. Donna Eden tells us that "…by tracing your meridians every day, you can direct the traffic in your energy transportation system. You can communicate to it in a language it understands…keeping the energies flowing along their natural routes."

On the following pages (see Figure 3, Daily Meridian Tracing Routine, pages 100 to 106) you'll find the Daily Meridian Tracing Routine which is a series of diagrams and instructions showing you how to trace your meridians. Please don't be put off by the lengthy explanations! I know it looks like you're going to have to embark upon a complicated marathon, but in actual fact, tracing your meridians only takes about *two minutes* to complete!

I recommend you get into the habit of practising this technique every morning before you get dressed. You'll not only begin to notice a difference in your energy levels, you'll also find the routine will help to keep you healthy and feeling good.

If you have an obvious problem around a particular meridian energy, like digestive problems (large and small intestine), you can trace that meridian several times a day if you wish.

Figure 3: Daily Meridian Tracing Routine

When you trace your meridians, use the palm of your hand (with your palm facing your body) to do the tracing. In this way, you're utilising your own electromagnetic energies to align the meridian's energies. Also, by using the whole of the flat of your hand, there's no question of you missing out bits of the actual meridian lines.

By the Law of Averages, you're going to hit the spot with one part of your palm or another!

The Central Meridian

Using your dominant hand, trace a straight line up the middle of your body from your pubic bone to your bottom lip.

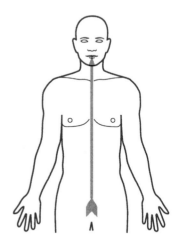

The Governing Meridian

Put one hand on your tail bone and trace up the middle of your back along your spine as high as you can reach. You'll get to a point where you can't move your hand any higher. When this happens, try to continue where you left off by reaching with the other hand over your shoulder with the intention of meeting the first hand so you can continue tracing this line up the centre of the back. (Don't worry if you can't get the hands to meet. Simply imagine they can and just visualize your hand continuing to trace the line.) With the second hand, carry on tracing the meridian up the neck, over the top of your head, down your nose, and finish at your top lip.

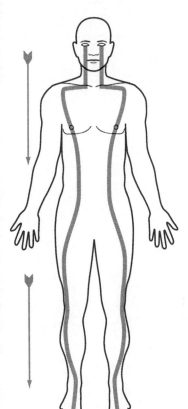

The Stomach Meridian

Using both hands, place them under the eyes and trace a straight line down your face to your collarbone. Move the hands out slightly and then bring them down straight over your breasts and down to your waist. Come in at your waist and then out at your hips. Then bring the hands straight down your legs and off the second toes of each foot.

The Spleen Meridian

Use both hands and start at the outside corner of each big toe. Trace lines up the inside of your legs, moving outwards at your hips. Trace up the middle of your rib care until you reach a point slightly above each nipple. Trace down the sides of the body to the bottom of the ribcage.

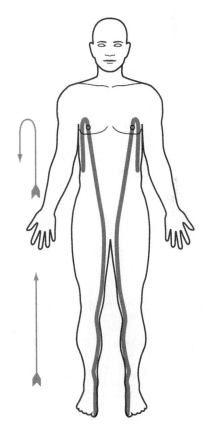

Finding the River

The Heart Meridian

Place one hand under the opposite armpit and trace a line from there right down the arm to your little finger and off. (Make sure you trace the line in alignment with your little finger.) Repeat opposite side.

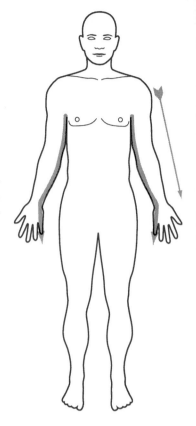

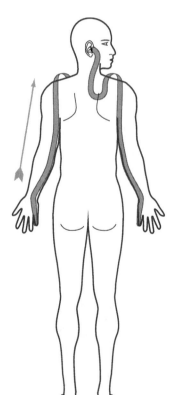

The Small Intestine Meridian

With one palm facing downwards, use the other hand to trace a line from the little finger of that hand up the outside of the arm and up to your shoulder. When you get there, push "the line" over to the back of your shoulder, then up towards the face, over the cheekbone and back towards the opening in your ear. Repeat opposite side.

Finding the River

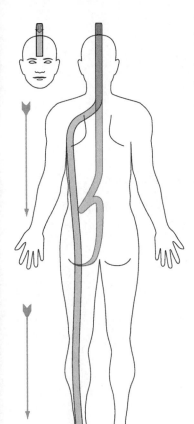

The Bladder Meridian

With the left hand, start in between the eyebrows and trace up and over the crown and down the neck. Bring the hand down as far as it will go and then reach behind you to continue tracing the line along the inside of the left side of the back. Trace over the buttocks, down the leg and calf, and off the little toe.

Now come back up to your brow centre and again trace back over head and down your neck. Bring the hand down as far as it will go and then reach behind you to continue tracing the line, but this time only trace it to just below your waist. Make a sharp hairpin bend upwards and back down again before finishing at the back of your left buttock. (If you can't reach back behind you high enough to continue tracing the line without "breaking it', trace it in your mind in the space where you can't reach.

The Kidney Meridian

Using both hands, place your middle fingers under the ball of each foot in line with the space between the big toe and the second toe. Drag your fingers back up along the inside of each foot and trace a circle around each inside ankle bone. Carry on straight up the inside of the legs, up the front of the body, and end at the points just underneath the collar bone.

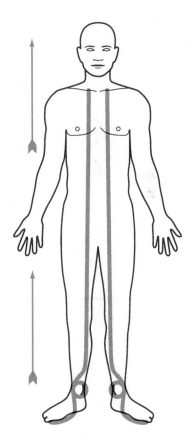

Finding the River

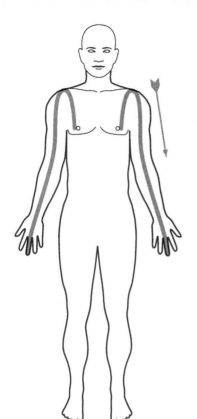

The Circulation–Sex Meridian

Place the fingers of one hand at the outside edge of the opposite nipple and trace a line up to the shoulder, down the inside of the arm, and off the middle finger. Repeat opposite side.

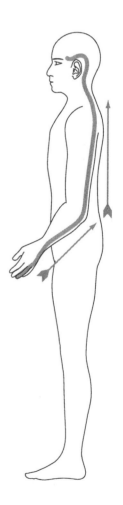

The Triple Warmer Meridian

With one palm facing the floor, use the other hand to trace up from the ring finger, up the back side of the arm, across the top of the shoulder, up your neck, around up the back of your ear, and over the top of it. Finish at the temple. Repeat opposite side.

The Gallbladder Meridian

Using the fingers of both hands, start tracing the line on the outside edge of the eyebrows. Pull the fingers back over the top of the ears. Trace up and forward to your forehead, back over the crown of your head, and down to your shoulders. Remove your hands from your shoulders and move them to the sides of your ribcage. Moving your hands downwards, trace forwards on the ribcage, snake back towards the waist, trace forward on the hips and then straight down the outsides of the legs and off the fourth toes.

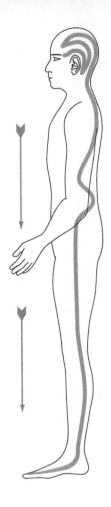

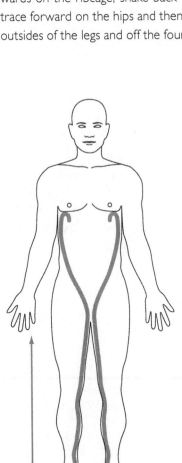

The Liver Meridian

Using both hands, place fingers on the outsides of the big toes and pull back to the ankles. Then trace up the insides of the legs, steering wide at the hips, up the sides of the ribcage, and back underneath your breasts, finishing in line with your nipples.

The Lung Meridian

Place your right hand over your left lung, trace up and over the shoulder and down the inside of your arm, and off your thumb. Repeat opposite side.

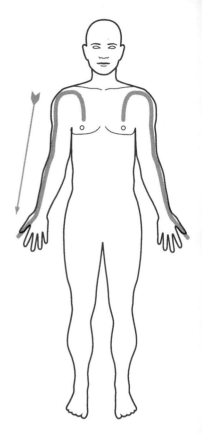

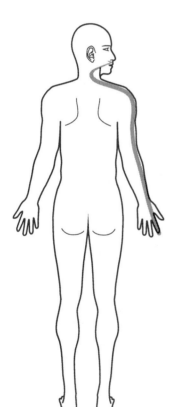

The Large Intestine Meridian

Place the fingers of one hand on the index finger of the other and trace straight up the arm towards the shoulder. Trace across the neck and on to the upper lip underneath the nose and out again slightly as if you were tracing the outline of a small moustache. Repeat opposite side.

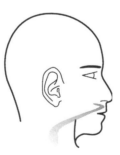

Head detail showing little mustache flick.

The Meridian Tracing in Figure 3 is from *Energy Medicine Techniques* by Donna Eden with David Feinstein.

Another really helpful thing you can do is to flush a meridian that you know is out of balance. As Donna Eden says in her book, *Energy Medicine*, "Flushing the energy out of a meridian is like backwashing its filter. It is often useful to backwash a meridian before you strengthen it [by tracing it], because this clears it of energetic debris, leaving more space for fresh energy to enter." She goes on to say, "When you trace a meridian or flush it, the energies of your hands flush the meridian's energy."

For example, if you, like me, are asthmatic, it's a good idea to flush your lung meridian just before you trace it on a daily basis during your regular practise of tracing your meridians. It's an excellent preventative measure to take and provides good maintenance for that particular meridian. Exercise 33 describes how to do it.

Exercise 33: Flushing a Meridian

If the main organ or system of one of your meridians causes a temporary or ongoing problem, flushing is an excellent way of re-balancing and maintaining it.

Go back to pages 101–106 to find the diagram that relates to the meridian you've selected. Let's do the Lung Meridian as an example in this case:

On an in-breath, use your open palm to trace the Lung Meridian *once in the opposite direction that is indicated on the diagram.* Repeat on the opposite side. You might like to imagine that your hands are magnets which are drawing stagnant debris out of your lungs as you do this movement.

On the out-breath, shake your hands to flick off any energetic flack you've accumulated on your hands.

Then, trace the Lung Meridian *in the direction indicated on the diagram* **three times**. Do this with great intention and deliberation.

Because we live in such a polluted world, flushing the Lung Meridian regularly, even if there aren't any problems, is a good idea!

Exercise 33 is from *Energy Medicine* by Donna Eden with David Feinstein.

The movements in Exercise 34 can get your energies moving, clear your head, and help your body to rid itself of toxins which may have accumulated. This one's called the Spinal Flush.

Exercise 34: The Spinal Flush

In this exercise, you're working on flushing out the lymphatic system of your body. The lymph works with the immune system in defending the body against anything from a cold to a full-blown disease. Lymph is naturally pumped through the body when you exercise or generally move around, so if you lead a sedentary lifestyle, (and many of us become less active in winter), the lymphatic system is likely to get pretty clogged and this can have an adverse effect on every other system in your body. It can also become congested when you're ill, stressed or if you've been exposed to environmental pollutants like living or working in the heart of a busy city with lots of traffic and noise. The Spinal Flush will cleanse your lymphatic system by sending toxins to the waste removal systems of your body, clear your head and energise you. It's also very helpful to do it if you think you're going down with a cold.

The Spinal Flush works on the Neurolymphatic reflex points which run along either side of your spine and affect every one of your meridians. You're going to be massaging down this spinal area, which you can do using a simple gadget you can easily make for yourself as follows:

Creating your own massage device: This can be done cheaply and effectively by acquiring two fairly hard rubber balls (the sort of exercise balls used by dog-owners that can be purchased from your local pet store or veterinary surgeries are excellent ones to use.) Place the balls in the foot part of a sock and then knot the ankle bit of the sock tightly to keep the balls wedged firmly together. This makes an excellent makeshift massage appliance that you can use to knead down your spine on either side of the vertebrae from the top of your neck to just above the buttocks.

Method: Find yourself a nice flat wall devoid of pictures or other obstructions. Stand against the wall and place the balls behind the area of your neck where it connects with your back and the top of your shoulders. (There's a big bone there at the top of your spine just where it connects with the neck—that's the place to start.)

What you're going to do is to massage down either side of your spine from the top of it to the bottom, and in so doing, flush your lymphatic system and help your body to rid itself of toxins.

Now, lean hard against the balls so they're jammed between your body and the wall. You'll find that by doing this, you can exert a firm pressure on either side of your spine. Stand slightly on tiptoe with your knees a bit bent so you can move the balls up and down in this area, keeping whatever pressure is right for you. (Maintain a firm contact by leaning against the balls and the wall all the way through this exercise, otherwise the balls will fall to the floor!) With practise, you'll be able to inch the balls down your spine by just moving away from the wall a *fraction* to allow them to slip down to the next set of vertebrae.

You'll find you can manipulate the balls to roll up and down each section of your spine by bending and stretching the knees and rising up and down on the balls of your feet. It may sound complicated, but actually it won't take long for you to get the hang of it!

As you move the balls further down towards the centre of your back, you can adjust their position because they sometimes slip sideways a bit. Keep working all the way down until you get to the bottom of your sacrum (which is that flat bit of bone just above your buttocks.)

If you want, you can then repeat the whole process once more.

Please don't be tempted to substitute tennis balls for dog balls because they're not hard enough to do a good massage job.

You'll find some of the points are very painful in that kind of exquisite way you experience sometimes with a good massage. You know: "Aaaaargh! No, don't stop!" Sometimes really sore points cease being sore quite quickly as you massage them. Other sore areas may take a bit more time to ease. Be prepared to work on the sore areas, but be sensible, and if any are really, really painful (as sometimes happens), don't torture yourself! If you get into the habit of doing this every day, any extremely sore spots will gradually become less painful. You'll also find that the sore spots change and new ones show up which you may not have felt before. That's all perfectly normal.

This do-it-yourself version of Donna Eden's "Spinal Flush" technique was created by my Energy Medicine teacher, Madison King.

You could also do Spinal Flush with a partner who performs the massage by massaging on either side of your vertebra using their thumbs, knuckles or two fingers together, slowly working from the top of the neck down to the tail bone. On finishing, it's a good idea for your partner to sweep firmly and quickly down your spine three times with the flat of their hands as a nice way to end the massage. Spinal Flush with a partner is a wonderful way of giving each other some TLC—which never goes amiss.

When you begin to understand your body as an energy system, there is a lot you can do to help keep your energies flowing, which in turn will help you to maintain good health. Our bodies are constantly giving us feedback about how our systems are functioning, so anytime you want to know whether your subtle energies are running healthily, all you have to do is to ask yourself how you feel. "If you feel fabulous, they *are!* If not, *they're not!*"*

If you'd like to learn more about working with your energies, balancing your meridians and your chakras, or ways to strengthen your aura and many more things besides, you'll find a wealth of information in the books written by Donna Eden (see the Further Information and Suggested Reading section at the back of the book). You can learn all kinds of simple energy techniques—from using acupressure points to disperse energy blocks to quick and easy energy exercises—which can strengthen and harmonise your energy systems and help with various problems.

Having seen Donna Eden at a workshop she was teaching in England a few years back, I can tell you that the energy and vitality she exudes is

---

* From *Energy Medicine* by Donna Eden with David Feinstein.

extraordinary. She puts this down to the benefits of the Energy Medicine techniques she has researched and developed and she's a living testament to its healing and health-giving qualities. I myself have been using a number of her techniques for several years now and have found them absolutely invaluable for helping to ward off illness, keeping my energies humming and refreshing and revitalising the body and mind.

Chapter 12

Energy Transformations

There are many different ways of working with Energy Medicine and I'd love to be able to tell you about them all, but there's only space to tell you about one other technique so that simply *has* to be the therapeutic energy healing modality called EmoTrance.

EmoTrance was created by another well-known innovator and pioneer in Energy Medicine, Silvia Hartmann. It's beautifully simple and easy to use and it's an indispensable tool for releasing worry, sadness and fear, and generally helping with relationship and love pain, past hurts and other emotional wounds. The technique is designed "...to repair things, unblock channels and pathways, restore some basic survival functions for the energy body and to give it the nutrition and care it always needed to grow."*

It's also a great way of becoming more aware of your own energy!

Exercise 35 introduces you to EmoTrance and helps you get a feel for it.

Exercise 35: Learning to Follow with Intention

You can do this on your own or with a partner.

Touch or have your partner touch you lightly with one fingertip on the arm or some other part of your body. Let yourself open up wholeheartedly to allow the feeling and sensation of that touch into your body.

Stay with that for a moment or two.

Then, either you or your partner lightly massage or tap the area.

As you experience this deeper touch, follow the sensation of it with conscious awareness as it travels through you.

Repeat this on different parts of your body until all touch and sensation flow instantly and smoothly and you can feel the energy moving through you.

You're feeling your inner rivers!

Practising this exercise can greatly enhance your sex life!

Exercise 35 is an EmoTrance exercise by Silvia Hartmann.

---

* From *Oceans of Energy: The Patterns and Techniques of EmoTrance*, by Silvia Hartmann PhD.

Everything is energy and the nature of energy is to *flow!* Think of it in terms of Nature. A river starts by rising up from its source as a small trickle, then it flows out and becomes a stream that turns into a river that then empties itself out into the sea. In the same way, your energy—just like a river—arises from its source (i.e., the Universe), flows into you, through you, and needs to flow *out* again. There's a constant circulation of Chi moving through us.

But sometimes it gets stuck and this can come about from holding onto any kind of emotion. This happens because the experience connected with those emotions has created a disturbance in the energy system. This disturbance causes us to develop emotional problems together with blocks and resistances of all kinds. Silvia Hartmann calls this syndrome the "pressure-cooker effect" and explains that "...the energy builds up and up and when it reaches a certain threshold, it turns into a physical sensation, then into a pain."

Have you ever noticed how we often use metaphors to describe emotional pain? For example: we say things like: "It feels like a great weight round my neck", or we talk about having "a gut feeling about something", and so on. The reason for this is that our emotional problems can cause sensations felt in the physical body which have no physical basis. And these physical feelings are simply feedback signals from the energy system. Those weights round the neck and the gut feeling aren't really physical at all. They're simply descriptions of blocked energy.

With EmoTrance, you can use those physical feelings to not only get in touch with your energy, but locate where the block is situated. And having done that, you can use your creative imagination (which is also energy!) to visualise the block, transform it, move it, let it flow and let it go!

How good is that?

Exercise 36 explains how easy it is to work with EmoTrance and let go of emotional pain.

Exercise 36: Emotional Healing

Recall an old emotion you know well and which you can feel in your body.

Ask yourself: Where do I feel this in my body? Place your hands where you can feel it and give it all your attention. (What you're feeling is the energy block caused by that emotion.)

Ask yourself: how does this energy feel? Does it feel tense? Heavy? Hot? Cool?

Remind yourself that it's only energy and that energy needs to flow!

Now, as you focus on that energy sitting there in your body, think about where that energy might like to go. (Energy can leave the body from any part of you—your ear, your toes, your skin or your right thumb!)

Stroke the area with your hands as if you were stroking a cat. This will help it to move. As you do this, imagine that energy softening, softening and beginning to flow out of you through the energy pathways—wherever they may be—all the way through you and out of you. Encourage it to flow in whatever direction it chooses to go.

Don't question how it moves and flows. Just accept that it's happening and allow it to do so.

Remind yourself again of this old emotion and go back to the place in your body where you first felt it to check how it feels.

Keep repeating the above process and continue with softening the energy and encouraging it to flow. Keep doing this until it moves out of your body quickly and easily.

You'll know when it's disappeared completely because you'll feel very different. There may be a sense of relief, a pleasurable surge of energy coursing through you, or a lightness of being. This is known as the "energised end state".

That's EmoTrance!

Exercise 36 is an EmoTrance exercise created by Silvia Hartmann.

Simple isn't it? And so effective! I really want to encourage you to get into the habit of using EmoTrance whenever you need it. Just remember, any hurt, anger, resentment, sadness or despair, etc., tells us that some part of the energy system is injured. So, in order to heal, all you need to do is to work with the physical sensation caused by that emotion, soften and flow and let it go. In this way, you *transform* the pain to a point where it's no longer there. EmoTrance is all about energy transformation!

By the way, any *good* feelings of joy, vitality, happiness and well-being, etc., are also telling us something about our energy systems. They're telling us we're aligned with the energies of the Universe, they're signalling we're in good shape and working well!

Exercise 37 (page 114) from Silvia Hartmann is a wonderful healing visualisation technique conjuring the image of energy falling like rain into our energy systems to heal and soothe. This exercise isn't about directing Chi through our bodies but about using imagery to "magically" summon outside energy to come to our aid.

She calls this "Innocent Energy" and sees it to be like soft rain falling. Because rain is totally neutral, it falls upon all things without judgement and without conditions. As an energy, it's neither good nor bad, but utterly benign and not to be confused with Chi Energy or concepts of calling in the Light or other well-known ways of healing.

Exercise 37: Evoking Innocent Energy

Spend a short while following your breath and imagining yourself lifting up lightly with each in-breath.

When you feel ready, call up the Innocent Energy. Imagine it falling all around you and inside of you like warm, gentle, summer rain. This rain is absolutely the softest and gentlest rain you've ever felt.

As it falls, both in you and all around you, notice how it flows through every part of you—your bones and muscles and tendons, your veins, arteries and vital organs, and through all your subtle energy channels; it even moves through the connective tissue that surrounds all these areas. Imagine it falling gently, flowing through you, washing away all the old thoughts and burdens you no longer need.

This Innocent Energy keeps falling all around you and in you for as long as you want it to do so. It's not addressing any particular issues or emotions or problems, it's simply moving through you, clearing and refreshing you, "…gentling and taking what it needs to take."

When you feel you have done enough, look up towards the Innocent Energy and give it your thanks. Then slowly open your eyes.

You should feel very clear and refreshed after doing this.

Doing the Innocent Energy exercise is also a very good way of finishing off any Emo-Trance work you've done on yourself, or for general energy rebalancing.

Exercise 37 is an EmoTrance exercise by Silvia Hartmann.

You can use this exercise as a preparation before using EmoTrance on yourself, as a way to help the "soften and flow" process to get underway if the energy feels really stuck, or as a way of conducting some effective healing in its own right.

You see, sometimes we hold emotional blocks in our energy systems which are so deep and traumatic, they're really hard to touch, even with a technique as gentle and simple as EmoTrance. Silvia Hartmann says: "There are parts of our energy systems which are so reversed, so damaged and so chaotic that they need this innocent energy that seeks no response, that makes no connection, that does not need to be channelled or processed in any way."*

In such cases, using this exercise is a very helpful first stage of healing that you can safely use on yourself. But if you are having a lot of difficulty working with a particularly painful emotion, please do seek the help of a qualified practitioner who'll be able to assist you in many more ways than I have room to describe here (see the Further Information and Suggested Reading at the back of the book to find an EmoTrance Practitioner).

* From *Oceans of Energy* by Silvia Hartmann PhD.

Finding the River

There are a number of different ways of applying EmoTrance and there is one in particular that centres on using it to give yourself some high grade energy nutrition.

Do you recall how in Chapter 8, we looked briefly at how energy is "food'? Since everything is energy, anything we give focus and attention to can be seen to be energetic "food". We "feed" on the energy of the people we mix with, the homes we live in, the work we do, the interests and hobbies we have, the places we frequent and the books, music, and films we like. But we need to choose our energy nutrition carefully as the energy of some things is more beneficial than the energy of others! We therefore need to do our best to select energy food that we know will keep us healthy and steer clear of energies that do the opposite.

Exercise 38 will teach you how to extract the greatest amount of energy nutrition from all kinds of things!

Exercise 38: Feasting on Energy

Bring to mind an object, person, plant, animal, landscape, music, work of art, or even some weather that makes you feel *really* good. If the object of your attention is physically there in front of you, then so much the better (but don't worry if it isn't).

Now, tune into its energy.

Let go of any resistance you may feel towards this energetic feast.

Ask yourself: Where do I feel this in my body?

Then ask yourself: Where does this energy need to go?

Direct it through your inner rivers. Help it to move all the way through you and out again.

Let it in! Let it flow! Then let it go!

Enjoy!

Exercise 38 is an EmoTrance exercise by Silvia Hartmann.

Exercise 39 (page 116) is an exercise that focuses on the heart. The heart is the place where we tend to feel so many emotions. Not only is it the seat of any pain, fear, anger and sadness we may hold, but also the place where we experience those positive emotions of joy, ecstasy, peace, tranquillity and feeling your connection to all things. It's therefore a very important part of ourselves and deserves to be given special care and attention.

When we think of a hurtful memory and re-experience the emotional pain that brings, we know how deeply and terribly wounded we can feel. But we forget that we're also capable of inflicting terrible hurt upon ourselves!

Just take a moment to consider how often you think badly of yourself. Ask yourself how often you judge and criticise *your* abilities, actions and ideas. If you heard someone speaking to another person in the way you sometimes speak to yourself, wouldn't you think they were being very unkind? Or cruel?

When you think of the pain we cause ourselves, as well as the pain caused by others, you can see how much the heart suffers. We need to gentle the heart, so that it can open to healing, forgiveness and love from ourselves to ourselves. We need to give healing to our own hearts and allow kindness, understanding and compassion to flow through us and out again.

Silvia Hartmann says, "It's structurally impossible to feel vibrantly happy and to think suicide, to feel love and think hatred or revenge, to be joyous and think sad thoughts. Intelligence, insight and creativity are all at their very peak when there are mental states of clarity and connectedness, when everything flows cleanly and a person is absolutely grounded in their own selves, and in the here and now.'

The following exercise is both supportive and nourishing and helps you to heal your heart any time you feel sad, or afraid or lonely.

Exercise 39: Heart Healing Exercise

"Don't underestimate the apparent simplicity of this exercise. Remember, the most powerfully effective principles in this world have a habit of being extremely simple, and the theory and practise of Heart Healing are an example of this.'*

Place both your hands on your own heart as this helps you to focus and concentrate your intention on what you're about to do. Then follow the instructions given in the poem below. You might like to read them out loud as you do so.

I put my healing hands
On my heart of energy
To heal what was once broken
To make right what once went wrong
To soften and to flow
To restore the Even Flow
So that my heart of energy
Can once again
Shine like the sun

Hold your hands on your heart for as long as you want (it can be just for a couple of minutes if that's what feels right). Then, when you're ready to finish the exercise, take a big breath in and a big breath out, and come back to ordinary awareness.

Exercise 39 is an EmoTrance exercise by Silvia Hartmann.
*From *Living Energy—The Patterns and Techniques of EmoTrance, Vol. 2,* by Silvia Hartmann PhD.

Exercise 39 is wonderful for giving yourself some very deep TLC. As Silvia Hartmann says: "(It) makes sure that your heart receives true love at last, which is what it really needs to heal...When you address your own heart directly and give it your own love, you will be giving true healing, which is what your heart needed all along and you will be twice empowered by being both the giver as well as the receiver."

There are many more ways of working with EmoTrance and further information can be found on the EmoTrance website or by reading Silvia Hartmann's books on the subject (see Further Information and Suggested Reading at the back of this book). A list of accredited practitioners can also be found on the website.

I really want to encourage you to get into the habit of using the EmoTrance technique of "soften and flow" on any emotional problems—both large and small—from your past and present. As you grow more aware of the clear communication between the emotions and the body you'll begin to be more in tune with how this mechanism is an effective early warning system telling you about some stuck energy and emotions in your Energy Body. The more you work with this, the more conscious you'll be of your inner feelings and the more grounded you can become.

EmoTrance is very empowering and it's the most wonderful tool to have whenever you're hacking your way through the jungle of your emotions! It's such a quick, easy and effective way of helping yourself, you may end up wondering how you ever managed before!

Chapter 13

Energy Psychology and Emotional Freedom

Energy Medicine and the related field of Energy Psychology have both evolved as a result of blending Western therapies with Eastern understandings of the subtle energy system. It was the East that discovered the knowledge about the energy anatomy all those thousands of years ago; however, it's now the turn of the West to lead the way, and it's doing so by developing the groundbreaking energy techniques which are set to become the cutting edge therapies of the future.

The term "Energy Psychology" describes a wide range of psychological techniques which combine different ways of working with aspects of the subtle energy system; e.g., the Chakras (the energy centres), the Aura (the systems of energy which surround the physical body), and the Meridians (the energy pathways and their related acupoints.)

The groundwork was laid for the evolution of this new field of Energy Medicine back in the early 1970s. At this time there was a growing interest amongst key people in the therapeutic world about Chinese Medicine and the workings of the meridian system.

This paved the way for the exploration and development of new energy-based therapies which began to appear. Notable amongst those was the system of Applied Kinesiology (AK). This was a diagnostic system developed by the American Chiropractor, Dr George Goodheart, which treated energy and body function through a combination of muscle testing and understandings of Chinese Medicine.

Another chiropractor, called Dr John Thie (who worked closely with Goodheart for a number of years), developed a system called Touch For Health, which was a blend of acupressure, touch and massage designed to improve posture and restore natural energy.

In due course, the work of Goodheart and Thie began attracting the interest of various people in the world of Psychology. Amongst these was Dr John Diamond, an Australian Clinical Psychiatrist, who had also studied AK and discovered the link between the meridians and the emotions. He started using a combination of psychiatry with AK and went on to develop a new field of psychotherapy that he called Behavioural Kinesiology (BK).

Another key player who came on the scene at this time was Dr Roger Callahan, a cognitive psychologist, who had studied BK briefly with John Diamond. Callahan later went on to discover an incredible technique that was to change the traditional face of psychology forever.

Dr Callahan's discovery came through his work with one of his patients, Mary, who was terrified of water. Her problem was long-standing and although Callahan had been working with her for some time, he'd made little headway. In one of her sessions, she happened to mention that the very thought of water made her feel sick in the pit of her stomach. Having recently been studying the meridian system, Callahan suddenly thought of asking her to tap on the point on her face that connected with the stomach meridian whilst holding on to the feelings she described. Almost immediately, her expression cleared and she declared that her problem had gone! To his complete astonishment, she then ran out of the room and into the garden towards his swimming pool, where she began dipping her hands into the water and splashing her face.

Inspired and enthused, Callahan continued working with Mary along these lines. This resulted in him developing an extraordinary technique that blended psychology with tapping on acupressure points which he called Thought Field Therapy (TFT).

Over a period of time he created a series of precise tapping combinations to deal with conditions like anxiety and addictions. He also created other individually tailored tapping sequences, depending on a person's particular problem. By utilising the link the meridians provided between body, mind and emotions, he had found a way of reaching into the energetic core of many people's emotional difficulties. In so doing, he bypassed the traditional requirement of lengthy therapy, and instead gave people the possibility of finding much quicker relief from their problems.

Energy Psychology was born!

TFT is one of the meridian-based Energy Psychology therapies and has since spawned the development of many other similar methods such as Be Set Free Fast (BSFF), Neuro Emotional Technique (NET), and Tapas Acupressure Technique (TAT), to name but a few. However the most well known "cousin" of TFT is Emotional Freedom Technique (EFT), and it is this system on which I will focus in this chapter.

EFT was developed from TFT by Gary Craig, one of Roger Callahan's students. Craig devised a simplified method of tapping that eliminated the complexities of TFT and created one short, easy sequence that could be used across the board on all kinds of different problems.

Now, you may be wondering why I'm telling you about a psychological technique when this is supposed to be a self-help book! Well, you see, Energy Psychology techniques, including EFT, can be used as therapeutic methods in their own right, or in tandem with other therapies, or as a self-help tool for *managing one's emotions!*

Dealing with our emotional problems can sometimes be quite difficult, as I'm sure you're aware! It often entails making changes in lifestyle, environment and relationships, or the need to find a new attitude, or the desire to let go of a limiting belief. And this can feel daunting, if not downright impossible at times! Making changes of any sort in our lives feels scary for many of us, because change can be frightening. Sometimes we'll do anything rather than jump in and take whatever action is required. Often we know exactly what we *need* to do but are scared rigid of *doing* it! How can we find a way to get past that fear?

There are the times when we feel completely stuck and we can't see the wood for the trees. Occasionally, we reach a state of complete overwhelm when we don't know where we are or how to begin to find a way through a problem. How can we help ourselves when we feel that way?

What do we do when we feel anger, hurt or resentment towards someone and it's eating us up? How do we manage when everything seems such a struggle and exhaustion and hopelessness set in? What can we do when worry or fear about the past, the present or the future rises up in our waking hours and disturbs our sleep at night? How can we cope with all the blips and crunches of everyday life when the pressure and stress get too much?

We all go through these times, usually with gritted teeth, frequently needing help but not knowing where to go for it or even wanting to admit that we might *need* help! Often we try to soldier on in ways which have long since proved ineffective but we repeat the patterns anyway because we don't know what else to do. Sometimes we find ourselves trying to cope by resorting to drugs, alcohol or food to bolster up our sagging self esteem, our exhaustion and our anxieties.

The good news is that it doesn't have to be this way!

EFT is a quick, easy and often permanent way of finding relief from emotional problems. You can help yourself deal with all sorts of mega, major or minor wobbles. It's a bit like a form of emotional clutter-clearing! EFT allows us to clear the channels of energy within us, dissolve the problems, lighten up and start seeing a way forward! Sometimes, it doesn't matter if you don't have the ultimate solution to your problem, just changing your attitude and seeing things in a different light can often herald the beginning of finding a way out of the jungle.

EFT can help you to move through problems like: anxiety, phobias, anger, jealousy, sadness and depression, low self-esteem, limiting beliefs, relationship difficulties, and performance issues. It's also been found to be very effective in dealing with some physical problems as well.

I'm going to show you how to work with it because I think it's an incredibly useful and effective method of helping oneself out of all kinds of emotional turbulence. Don't be put off by the lengthy explanations. Just take your time to read through the directions and then, once you get the hang of it, you can zoom through a sequence in a matter of minutes and really start making a difference to your life.

Let's start taking a look at what it's all about:

"Emotional Freedom Technique is like a form of emotional acupuncture, except we don't use needles" (Gary Craig). By tapping a short sequence of acupressure points on the skin whilst at the same time focussing on a remembrance that brings up an unwanted or negative emotional response, we can, believe it or not, actually shift the brain's reaction to a particular issue. It's as though a kind of re-wiring takes place that can completely remove the original emotional intensity associated with the problem. In other words, you can still remember the cause of the problem but it no longer triggers hurt or discomfort. A lot of research is currently being conducted into exactly how this happens, but there's massive and overwhelming anecdotal evidence from therapists and those who have tried it on themselves that EFT actually does what it says on the tin!

Gary Craig's "discovery statement" is that, "All negative emotions are a direct result of disturbances within the energy system."

Previously, the traditional therapeutic view was that the actual thought or memory was the "fuse" that set off the negative emotion. However, it's now understood that *between* the thought or memory comes the *disturbance*, that *then* triggers the emotional response. It's a bit like what would happen if you took the back off your TV and poked around inside with a screwdriver. There'd be a disruption to the wiring and the result would be a distortion of the screen images. The same thing happens between the memory and the negative emotional response. Your energy system is "screwdrivered" when a disturbance pops up and disrupts it. This can trigger just about any negative emotion there is.

So, what we're doing with EFT is working with the *emotion* and not the *memory*. By cutting to the core of how you *feel*, rather than focussing on all the history surround the issue, the time required for dealing with the problem automatically becomes a great deal shorter!

Although with this technique, we're working on the meridians (we looked briefly at this subject in Figure 3, The Daily Meridian Tracing Routine (pages

100–106), it's not necessary for you to have an in-depth understanding of the system in order to do EFT. So don't worry, you don't have to take a foundation course in Acupuncture before you start! There are books listed in the Further Information and Suggested Reading section at the back of the book that will give you much more detailed information about all aspects of EFT than I can provide here. I thoroughly recommend that you read the book co-authored by Donna Eden, David Feinstein and Gary Craig—because it's not only very informative but also gives an overview of how Energy Psychology and Energy Medicine both relate to and complement each other—and also Silvia Hartmann's books on EFT for innovative ways to work.

EFT Tapping Sequence

There are two sequences of tapping used in EFT. One is called the "Long Form" and was the first sequence developed by Gary Craig. This is still used by some people and is often particularly effective for dealing with traumatic events. However, the other sequence, or "Short Form', was developed within the last few years and is now more widely used. I've found it to be equally effective and more user-friendly than the longer version, and it's this form that I'm going to teach you.

However, before I explain the sequence of tapping positions, I just want to give you a few pointers about tapping:

- Most people prefer to tap with their dominant hand, but you can use the non-dominant one if you prefer
- Tap firmly, but never so hard that you'll bruise or hurt yourself
- Tap each point between 5 to 7 times before moving on to the next position in the sequence
- It doesn't matter which side of your body you tap. You can even switch sides half way through if you like!

You'll find all the tapping points illustrated in Figure 4 (page 124), and, incidentally, these points cover all the meridian endings. You might like to refer to this as you go through the list below:

Karate Chop (KC)

The KC is the fleshy bit on the outside edge of the hand that you'd use to hit someone or something with a karate chop. Bring the index, middle and fourth fingers of one hand together to form a small broad pad and tap on the KC area of the other hand (this way you can be sure of covering the meridian.) Most people prefer to do the tapping with their dominant hand. For example, if you're right handed, you'd use your right hand to tap against the KC position on the left hand.

Figure 4: A Quick Guide to Using EFT

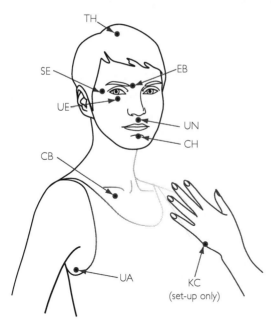

Key to Tapping Points

Karate Chop	=	KC
Top of the Head	=	TH
Eyebrow	=	EB
Side of the Eye	=	SE
Under the Eye	=	UE
Under the Nose	=	UN
Chin	=	CH
Collar Bone	=	CB
Under the Arm	=	UA

Once you've decided what problem to tap on—*calibrate* (i.e., score the intensity of your emotions on a scale of 0–10 with zero meaning there is no intensity and 10 meaning the emotion is at the highest intensity). If it's fairly high it might be anything from 8–9; and if it's moderate it might be around 5–7. Low intensity would be around 3–4, and minimal intensity would be anything from 0.25–2.

Create a Set Up Statement: This could be something such as, "Even though I'm really angry with my boss, I deeply and completely love and accept myself."

Repeat the Set Up Statement: Repeat the statement three times whilst continuously tapping the Karate Chop (KC).

Formulate a Reminder Phrase: This is a shortened version of the Set Up Statement, e.g., "Angry with my boss."

Repeat the Reminder Phrase: Say it out loud as you tap through each position of the Sequence (or Round), remembering to tap between 5 to 7 times on each point as follows:

> TH = "Angry with my boss."
> EB - "Angry with my boss."
> SE = "Angry with my boss."
> UE = "Angry with my boss."
> UN = "Angry with my boss."
> CH = "Angry with my boss."
> CB = "Angry with my boss."
> UA = "Angry with my boss."

This example shows **one Round** (i.e., one round of the sequence of tapping points).

You need to do **two Rounds** (i.e., one following immediately after the other).

Then:

- Take a big breath
- Calibrate
- Check what's changed for you intensity-wise and note the score
- The intensity should reduce with each round you tap

When you get down to a score of four or lower, make a slight alteration to the wording of the Set Up Statement to reflect the changes in your emotional intensity; e.g., "Even though I'm still a bit angry, I deeply, etc…"

You'll also need to change the Reminder Phrase accordingly; e.g., "Still a bit angry."

When the intensity gets to two or lower, change the Set Up Statement again to reflect this; e.g., "Even though I'm a tiny bit angry, I deeply, etc…"

Also change the Reminder Phrase again; e.g., "Tiny bit angry."

Keep repeating the whole thing with a Set Up Statement followed by two rounds of the Sequence whilst noting the changes in calibration. Keep doing this till you reach an emotional calibration of zero intensity

> *Don't be tempted to stop working simply because the intensity has gone down very low and you're feeling better. You need to get the intensity on a problem down to a zero before moving on to something else, otherwise it'll show up again at some point.*

Most problems have more than one aspect to them. For instance, in the above example, once you've dealt with your feelings of anger against your boss, you may recognise another aspect arising which is around your anger towards yourself for allowing your boss to upset you so much. If this is the case, then you need to tap on feeling angry with yourself; i.e., calibrating the intensity of your feelings, choosing a Set Up statement, tapping on this three times, beginning on the KC, and then going on to do two rounds of the Sequence. Once again, the whole exercise needs to be repeated from top to bottom until you've got the feelings down to zero.

In some situations, even further aspects may arise. This is when you find out how good EFT is at dissolving layers of emotions very quickly and revealing the root causes of various problems. This is very clarifying and helpful. Without a technique like EFT, we often find it very hard to see these subconscious issues and, as a result, we don't manage to heal and overcome our difficulties.

If further aspects arise, treat each one individually in exactly the same way and continue to tap till you get it down to zero.

Top of the Head (TH)

The TH is the area in the centre of the crown of the head directly in line with your ears. Use *all* the fingers of one hand to tap this point. Many meridians pass through this area and if you use all your fingers to tap here you can be sure of covering every one of them!

From now on, all the points are tapped using just the index and middle fingers of your hand. Using two fingers rather than one ensures you're going to hit the right area!

Beginning of the Eyebrow (EB)

At the beginning of the eyebrow just above the nose.

Side of the Eye (SE)

On the bone of the eye socket around the outside of the eye.

Under the Eye (UE)

On the bone of the eye socket just under the eye

Under the Nose (UN)

On the area just under your nose and above your top lip.

Chin (CH)

Midway between the point of the chin and underneath your bottom lip.

Collar Bone (CB)

Just underneath your collar bone and above the first rib (find the U-shaped hollow between your collarbones, move down about an inch and slightly to the side).

Under the Arm (UA)

About 4 inches under the arm on a level with the nipple (for men) or the seam of your garment or bra (for women). Some people find this area feels quite tender.

If you've been using your right hand to tap from your head downwards on the right hand side of your body, you'll find that you'll need to tap underneath the left arm when you get to the UA point.

You might like to practise tapping through this sequence a few times starting with TH and finishing at UA (leave the KC for the time being). This will help you to familiarise yourself with what's known as "The Sequence". (I know the tapping may seem a bit of a whacky thing to do, but remember, you'll be doing this in the privacy of your own home and not out in public!) It's not difficult to do and it's really very easy to remember as you simply start at the top of the head and just move on down.

Once you've gone through the tapping sequence a few times, just leave it for the moment and read on while I explain more about how to work on a problem using EFT.

1. You need to identify and name your problem; e.g., this anger towards my boss, this fear of public speaking, this worry about my exams, this lack of work, this headache, this fear of birds, this dislike of my body, etc. Write down the problem you've decided to work on.

2. You need to calibrate (measure) the intensity around this emotion on a scale of 0 to 10, with 0 equal to no intensity at all and 10 equal to the highest intensity you could feel. Write the intensity score down beside the name of your problem.

   Remember, we're only interested in the emotions and feelings you have about this. Logic and rationality don't come into it! Emotions are mostly not logical!

   Let's use the example of being angry with your boss to help you get started. And let's suppose the intensity of this feeling is measured at a 10.

3. You need to formulate a "Set Up" statement, which should always be made in the negative because problems involve negative thinking. Basically, this statement describes the problem and how it makes you feel and always starts with the words "Even though..." This is standard procedure for any problem no matter what the issue is.

   The Set Up statement in our example would therefore be: "Even though I'm really angry with my boss..."

   The purpose of the Set Up Statement is to help deal with any unconscious negative thinking and limiting beliefs getting in the way of letting go of the problem at hand. The official name for this kind of thing happening is "Psychological Reversal" (PR).

   PR is a problem that most of us have encountered from time to time; e.g., we want to lose weight, but instead we either stay the same size or pile on more pounds! Or we say we want to de-clutter our home but somehow never really seem to get started.

   This happens because somewhere in the subconscious there's a deep-seated (and often completely hidden) emotional reason for not following through on your desired action. In the case of the weight-loss example, it might be because deep down you're worried that by becoming slimmer and fitter, you'll provoke envy in others, or that you'll feel deprived at the thought of having to give up certain favourite foods. In the case of the clutter-clearing, the inability to de-clutter might be about an underlying fear of having to throw out objects to which emotional and sentimental value is attached, or to do with the fact that on a subconscious level you may be finding some emotional safety and security in the clutter itself.

PR is almost always present in most physical complaints, and is frequently the root cause of self sabotage. You can see this happening to yourself or others when repeated efforts to make changes in some area of life always seem to be thwarted for no apparent reason. Many people try to overcome it with the use of will power and don't understand why they keep failing. Now you know it's to do with being psychologically reversed about the issue! As one of my astrology teachers used to say, "The unconscious always wins!" Thankfully, EFT can help to get you past this problem.

4. You have to correct any possible PR by neutralising it in the Set Up statement. We do this by adding a positive affirmation to the Set Up statement about the negative emotion. It needs to state that *despite* these negative feelings, we can accept that this is how we feel and that we still love ourselves nevertheless.

   The positive affirmation you say is always the same and the standard phrase used by Gary Craig is: "I deeply and completely love and accept myself."

   Please note, if you don't feel comfortable saying "I deeply and completely love and accept myself," try saying, "I love and accept myself" instead. Or even "I accept that I'm feeling this way." The most important thing is that you state that you can *accept* your feelings—whatever they are—at this moment in time.

   The Set Up statement for our example might therefore go like this: "Even though I'm really angry with my boss, I deeply and completely love and accept myself" (or use one of the alternative affirmations suggested above).

5. You need to say the Set Up Statement out loud three times all the while tapping on the KC point

6. You need to decide on a short "Reminder Phrase". This is usually a shortened version of the Set Up Statement. This phrase is necessary to help you stay focussed on the problem, otherwise you might just tap and let your mind wander off onto other things!

In the case of our example, the reminder phrase could be: "Angry with my boss." Remember, it's important to stay focussed on the negative aspects of the problem. After all, if you weren't feeling negative about it, you wouldn't *have* a problem!

7. You need to tap through The Sequence (like you did earlier) only this time you're going to repeat the Reminder Phrase as you tap on each point. Going through this sequence of tapping is called a "Round" and you do two Rounds of the sequence every time.

8. When you've tapped through two Rounds, take a deep breath in, followed by a deep breath out. This gives you a chance to pause and take stock

9. Now, re-calibrate. Check whether the intensity on this issue has gone down. The objective is to get it down to a zero. Let's suppose it's gone down to a 7. (Always make a note of where the new calibration stands.) In this case, you'd repeat the whole process again from saying the Set Up statement three times (whilst tapping on the KC) and then going through two Rounds of the Reminder Phrase again. Don't forget, tap all the points in the sequence and say the same reminder phrase at each one just like you did before.

   Pause, breathe and score again. The intensity should have moved down even further.

10. Keep working in this way, prefacing every round by tapping on the KC and saying the Set Up statement three times followed by two Rounds of the reminder phrase. You should find the intensity of the problem comes down each time.

    When the intensity is down to a score of 4 or below, you need to change the Reminder Phrase to reflect the change. In the case of our example, you'd now say: "Still a bit angry."

    Take a big breath, and score again. If the intensity has gone down to a 2 or a 1, you need to change the reminder phrase again to reflect the lessening intensity and say instead: "Tiny bit angry."

    Once it's down to a zero, you then need to check your overall intensity to make sure it's really gone. Ask yourself: "When I think about how angry I feel about my boss, what's the intensity of my problem now?" Tap on any intensity still remaining to ensure that everything's subsided.

    If another aspect of the problem comes up (e.g., having dissolved the anger with your boss, you may find that you're actually pretty angry with yourself), then work on it in exactly the same way.

For a complete recap on all this information and guidance through the whole EFT tapping process (or Basic Recipe as it's known), turn back to Figure 4, A Quick Guide to Using EFT (page 124).

When you decide what issue you want to work on, you might like to keep this guide open in front of you to help you work your way through your problem.

Be persistent. Don't stop half way through because you're feeling better. If you do this, you run the risk of sweeping stuff under the carpet. Always aim to get it down to zero.

The EFT tapping process might sound very long-winded, but actually, you can work through a couple of rounds in just a few minutes. In many cases, it may not take you very long at all to completely dissolve an anxiety, a fear, a physical feeling, or whatever.

Trouble shooting

If the intensity doesn't come down, it's a good idea to ask yourself the following question and note down the answer: "What would happen if this problem wasn't there any more?" If you don't know the answer outright, just take a guess at what it might be.

Tap on what comes up and see if you can get the score down to zero. When you've done so, check to see how you're feeling. Then see if anything has shifted around your original Set Up Statement. Calibrate again and go back to tapping on that. You should find the intensity dissolves this time.

What you've learnt in this chapter is just a taster for what can be achieved with EFT. With practise, you can bring about many liberating changes and transformations in your life. It doesn't matter whether your emotional problems are linked to events long past, to present challenges or to anxiety about the future, they can all be helped with EFT. Please remember, however, that with more complicated issues it's always advisable to work with a therapist. And please consult your doctor for all medical or physical problems before using EFT (see Further Information and Suggested Reading at the back of the book for where to find a practitioner).

Some people worry that being released from the emotional intensity of a problem might somehow prevent them from benefiting from the "lessons" they could be learning from the situation. Don't worry about this! You'll still have the *memory* of the event that caused the problem. The difference is that it no longer causes any disabling emotion. EFT doesn't suppress unwanted emotional reactions. It simply releases them. This still allows room for understandings to take place and those all-important lessons of life to be learnt.

EFT is a wonderfully self-empowering technique that is easily learnt and can be applied to many problems without any difficulty. Try it on everything! Once you've got the hang of it, I'm sure you'll find it's a totally indispensable tool to have in your self-help box!*

---

* This chapter on EFT is provided as a good faith effort to expand the use of EFT in the world. It represents the ideas of Sally Topham and does not necessarily represent those of Gary Craig or EFT. Complete understanding of EFT and EFT training videos are available at www.emofree.com.

Part III

Seasonal Energies

Ways to Keep in Tune, Flowing and Connected

Chapter 14
Planting New Seeds

The ancient Celts lived very close to the land and revered Nature as their teacher. They saw within the seasons a reflection of man's own cycle of life from birth, to maturity and into death. Rituals were constructed around the natural phenomena connected with the movements of the sun and the earth, the solstices and equinoxes were celebrated as important turning points in the cycles of natural change, and they based their spirituality and philosophy upon their deep connection with the power and magic of Nature.

Today, we can still benefit from being guided by Nature just as much as our distant ancestors were. In fact, feeling our connection to the earth and all that's natural becomes even more vital in this fast technological age of the 21st century. We, too, can tune into the seasons and view them as metaphors for our own personal growth.

We all respond to the seasons, although for some of us, that may happen on a mostly unconscious level. But if we choose to become more aware of our own cycles, then little by little, we'll learn when to clear, plant, cultivate and harvest our energies. The process of growth is a process of motion. Nothing remains static. Things change and transform, things arise and are created, and things die away. It's a continuous cycle of seeds being planted, growth taking place, the blossoming of fruits and flowers, the harvesting of the crops and the dying back and deep sleep of winter.

By following the seasons, we have an *aide memoire* to remind us what we could be doing in terms of our personal unfolding at any time of the year. In Part III, I want to show you how to work on yourself by watching for Nature's seasonal cues. I'm going to help you make full use of the techniques I've been teaching you so far and also give you a few more strategies to help you on your way.

Spring

Spring is a time when Nature awakes after its long winter sleep and hibernation, and we begin to see gradual evidence of fresh growth and new life. Little by little, dawn creeps in earlier, and, in the Northern Hemisphere, daylight finally begins to stretch out beyond mid afternoon as the sun rises higher in the sky and brings us back into the light after the darkness of winter.

Early Spring begins in February; in fact, the Japanese always mark February 4th as the first day of this season. Even though we might have thick snow lying upon the ground or it's freezing cold, this is the time when there's a definite shift in the patterns of Nature. Personally, my energies are always given a boost by the carpet of crocuses and snowdrops which cover my lawn in early February. My heart lifts with all the promise in the air.

This is the time of year when we're surfacing from the effects of winter in ourselves. If we pay attention, the energies stirring outside of us are reflections of something similar happening within. All those new shoots which are still buried underground are struggling upwards towards the light. Early Spring is a time of re-adjustment and change, of emerging out of the withdrawal we've been in all winter. A re-birth is taking place. As we come out of the darkness and are drawn back into the light, the going can sometimes feel like too much hard work after months of more sedentary living. Many of us are struggling to uphold any New Year plans or resolutions which may have been made. More than likely, quite a lot of us have already given up on them! That plan to lose weight after the excesses of the festive season has possibly bitten the dust, maybe we've started to miss some of those evening classes we signed up for, and as for weeding through the files or doing some spring cleaning—forget it!

It's often hard to get the focus and intention going in Early Spring especially if one day is bright sunshine and the next day is icy cold, dreary and miserable. Our energy systems can become sluggish in winter. This causes the immune system to be weakened and makes us susceptible to coughs, colds and viruses. We may be toxic from negative thinking—remember how this can change your body's chemistry. We could also find ourselves suffering from a general feeling of apathy that may well have been exacerbated by the lack of sunshine or too much stodgy food over the previous months.

Whether you're suffering from Spring Malaise or you're full of energy and optimism, now's a really good time to turn back to Chapter 11 and remind yourself how to trace your meridians (pages 99–104). It will help get your energies moving and therefore allow you to be more aligned to the energy of the season. Whatever kind of space you're in emotionally and energetically "...tracing your meridians is one of the most effective ways...to keep the energy highways open, minimize the traffic jams, maintain the import and export systems, remove stagnant energy and bring in a fresh energy supply."* You can practise this simple technique easily before you get dressed in the mornings. I promise you it will help you to feel healthier, make a difference to your energies, and it will only take you a couple of minutes to do each day! Don't forget to flush any meridian that needs help as well!

---

* From *Energy Medicine* by Donna Eden and David Feinstein.

One other thing you should definitely do at this time of year is the Spinal Flush (page 106). Many of us become less active when it's very cold and that means our lymphatic system isn't working efficiently at clearing out the toxins. I can't recommend this practise highly enough! It's absolutely wonderful for clearing your energies. Do give it a try! Not only will it ease out the grungy points along your spine, but it'll clear your head and it's also a very helpful preventative measure to use if you think you're coming down with a cold.

Helpful Techniques for Spring

Here are a few other things to watch out for in Early Spring and ways you can help yourself:

Mood swings: Work with images which trigger your endorphins. Review Exercise 1 (page 4) and Exercise 2 (page 5), Exercise 3 (page 7), and Exercise 5 (page 13).

If you haven't already begun, start writing in your journal (see Chapter 4) and get your whinges, gripes, and irritations—and anything else you're feeling—down on the page in black and white. Believe me, it's better out than in!

Apathy or struggling to find the strength for new growth: Try EmoTrance (see Chapter 12). and ask yourself: "When I think about how I can't be bothered (or whatever it is you're feeling), where do I feel it in my body?" When you've identified the place, put your hands there. Then ask: "Where does this energy need to go?" Allow the energy to soften and flow and leave your body.

Move your body: Exercise, walking, and dancing will all keep those endorphins flooding your body and help you raise and maintain a more positive attitude. This will help you to further new plans and ideas. Get out in nature as it will lift your spirits and help you get into a better state of mind.

Check out your diet: Green is the colour of Spring so it's good to eat lots of green food. Green vegetables contain a lot of chlorophyll, which is especially good for the digestive tract and for encouraging the healing of wounds. They also contain vitamins C, E and A as well as calcium and B vitamins, which are good for stress.

Detox: Consider going on a detox regime (see Further Information and Suggested Reading at the back of book for additional information).

Spring Traditions

Many of the ancient Spring customs were about performing rituals for abundance. In Babylonia and Assyria for example, there were festivals to celebrate the planting of new crops centring on themes of renewal, creation and fruitfulness in which Ishtar, their Goddess of Love and Fertility was worshipped. As Ishtar's cult spread into Europe, her name changed and she became known by the Saxon name of Eostre. It's interesting, isn't it, that the Christian festival of Easter, that celebrates the resurrection of Jesus Christ, takes its name from this pagan goddess! In fact, the Easter festival does embody some of the old symbolism because, in essence, it repeats the theme of re-birth and new life. Its message is that we each have the possibility to be born anew, by letting go of the past and moving on.

The long-established Spring tradition of sowing new crops and cultivating the land therefore has great relevance to our personal growth. After all, we sow seeds in the form of our ideas and plans. Every time we want to make changes in ourselves or begin something new, we're planting new seeds. We can therefore make good use of the energies of this time to focus on trying to release unskilful patterns of thought and behaviour and to work on letting go of limiting beliefs. By weeding out things which hold us back from being who we really are, we can make ourselves more fertile for the cultivation of any new seeds we wish to plant within ourselves.

For many of us, this is the time of year when we're often enthused with ideas of new ventures and changes we could make in our lives. It may be that you're thinking of beginning new projects and entertaining various visions and dreams about what you want to do in both the long and the short term. There's a great sense of things thawing and opening up now, of hope, of a greening and budding. *This* is the time when we should be making our New Year resolutions, not on January 1st! The earth is being filled with new energy and we need to tune into this and allow it to carry us along.

So, what dreams or ideas are surfacing for you? What new things are arising within you which are waiting to be born? Where is your river taking you?

Building Confidence

New projects or plans often require the necessity of making changes and, as I said in Chapter 13, this can be scary or very uncomfortable for many of us. Is this something that happens to you? Do you find that when it comes to actually trying to get something new started, there's a part of you that backtracks, becomes bored, finds something else to do, or thinks it can't be bothered because it won't happen? Is there a part of you that's afraid of stepping out into the unknown or taking a leap of faith? Maybe you don't really feel you have much faith? Maybe you've had experiences in the past of telling people about some new plan or vision only to be totally demoralised by their negative reactions? Such responses can really make a dent in our confidence and self-esteem, especially if the put-down has come from a friend or relative.

If you're someone who lacks confidence and consistently find yourself short on support, encouragement and enthusiasm from others, here are three things you can do to change all that:

1. DON'T talk about your project to those people who you know won't support you (*you know who they are*).

2. INSTEAD, express your ideas safely and openly by writing in a journal about what you want to do. Use this process to expand on any further thoughts and feelings that come up. Journaling is great for helping our brains to sift through and process projects and ideas. It can also become a very creative practise.

3. USE EFT (see Chapter 13) to dissolve your feelings of lack of confidence and support as per the following example:

   a. **Calibrate:** score your feelings around this issue.

   b. **Create a Set Up statement:** such as "Even though I don't believe I can do this and neither does anyone else, I deeply and completely love and accept myself" (repeat 3 times).

   c. **Create a Reminder Phrase:** such as "Don't believe I can do this" and tap through two Rounds of the sequence on all the points.

   d. **Rating:** Take a breath and re-calibrate

   e. **Repeat:** Carry on tapping through however many Set Ups and Rounds of the sequence are required until you've got it down to zero.

   If any other blocks or resistance come up to taking some action on your project, then tap on those as well.

EFT is such a good way of getting rid of self-doubt and lack of confidence!

Comfort Zones

Another thing that comes up frequently when we're trying to start something new and make changes is the fear of stepping outside of our Comfort Zones.

Comfort Zones are mental and emotional boundaries we set for ourselves. They're based on limiting beliefs which keep us from stretching ourselves or taking risks. We hide behind these self-imposed parameters because we believe that doing so will keep us safe. Comfort Zones are one of the biggest causes of self-sabotage. They restrict our talents, possibilities and potential, and prevent us from finding success and fulfilment. This subconscious negative thinking can totally undermine any new plans, projects and ideas and keep us from being our true, authentic self.

Here are some examples of Comfort Zones. Have a look at them to get an idea of how to identify them in yourself.

1. You find yourself in a relationship that's going nowhere.
2. You're in a job that's hugely dissatisfying or stressful, or where you're not being recognised for your skills and talents.
3. Your relationship history shows predictable patterns; e.g., always ending up going for the same type of person. Even though the personalities of each of the people you've dated may have been totally different, you find that you've ended up with yet another lover who can't be emotionally present. Perhaps one of them was never at ease with any expression of emotion, another one might have disappeared when you went through a really bad time, and yet another, whilst able to stick around physically, had a drink or drug problem, so wasn't really there for you.
4. You've noticed that when it comes to getting promoted at work or getting another job, you never really seem to move forward. Perhaps you've made some changes in the past but they never turn out to be terribly significant and they haven't really helped you to move onwards and upwards.
5. You tend to get attracted to unattainable people in terms of relationships.
6. You never seem to get beyond a certain threshold with the money you earn.
7. You have a pattern of not finishing projects which you've started.

Repetitive situations in your life can signal that you're stuck in a Comfort Zone. Believe me, we've all got them! You need to recognise them and eradicate as many as possible. The paradox with most Comfort Zones is that they're not really *comfortable*, they're just *familiar*! And whilst that familiarity tends to make you feel safe, it doesn't help you to feel satisfied or fulfilled. It holds you back and suppresses your creativity, skills and talent. Ask yourself how many times you've allowed yourself to stay stuck because you're unwilling, for whatever reason, to try to move out of that place?

Exercise 40 will help you to recognize and eliminate Comfort Zones.

Exercise 40: Getting Out of a Comfort Zone

Important factors to remember:

1. You don't have to know why you've got a comfort zone to eradicate one! You simply have to recognise it!

2. Stay with your emotions and feelings about how scary it is to think of stepping out of this particular Comfort Zone and work with that issue either using EFT or EmoTrance. (see Chapter 12)

Here are a couple of examples to help you get going with this:

Example 1: Your current relationship is going nowhere but you can't find a way of extricating yourself.

- Score the emotional intensity and then EFT it:
- Set up suggestion: "Even though my relationship with (name of person) isn't going anywhere and I can't find it in myself to leave, I deeply and completely love and accept myself" (repeat three times).
- Reminder phrase: "Can't find a way to leave" (and tap through two Rounds of the sequence)
- Breathe and calibrate
- Keep tapping through setups and rounds of sequences until you get it down to zero.
- If any other aspects arise around this issue afterwards such as: I'm afraid of hurting him/her, I'm afraid I'll never find anyone else; supposing I'm just bored? etc., then tap on each of those too and get them down to zero.

Example 2: You want to earn more money but you never seem to manage it.

- Close your eyes and vividly imagine how you'd feel if you were earning 20% or 30% more than you are now.
- Use EmoTrance on whichever percentage makes you feel most uncomfortable.
- Ask yourself: "When I think about earning ___ % more, where do I feel that in my body?"
- Put your hands there. Know that you're feeling the energy of that emotion and that energy wants to leave your body.
- Ask yourself: "Where does this energy want to go?"
- Use your hands to stroke the energy in the direction it wants to take
- Let that place in your body soften, allow the energy to flow and let it go

Keep doing this until it's gone.

Laws of Attraction

In the early 1990s, a book came out by Deepak Chopra called *The Seven Spiritual Laws of Success* that was probably the precursor to all the Law of Attraction books which were to flood the market come the dawn of the new millennium. Chopra was one of the first people to transmit the idea of the quantum body–mind being part of the quantum universe to a worldwide audience. In this book Chopra tells us—amongst many other things—that there's no difference between our bodies and the body of the Universe because, "...at quantum mechanical levels there are no defined edges. You are like a wiggle, a wave, a fluctuation, a convolution, a whirlpool, a localised disturbance in the large quantum field. The large quantum field—the universe—is your extended body...(you can therefore) influence the energy and informational content of your extended body—your environment, your world—and cause things to manifest in it."

Chopra says that conscious change is brought about by *attention*, which energises, and *intention*, which transforms. Whatever we put our attention on—good or bad—will have the effect of causing that thing to grow stronger in our lives. So, if we put our attention on things we don't believe we can do, then more than likely we won't be able to do them! On the other hand, if we put our attention on things we want to do, (and believe we can do), we're almost certainly going to be able to manifest them in some way. Intention, he says, "triggers transformation of energy and information."

But before the action of consciously planting any new seed, we first have to have an idea of what it is we want to do. Everything that's ever been invented or was ever achieved was once an idea in someone's mind that became reality through the use of attention and intention. And one of the best ways of helping the mind to open up to its creative possibilities is to allow it to *dream!*

By allowing yourself to dream—without any expectations, but in a state of joyful play—you can open yourself to all kinds of possibilities and change.

Exercise 41 can help you with attracting your dream.

Exercise 41: The Magic Wand

Imagine you've got a magic wand. One flick of it will bring you any opportunity you could imagine and anything you need to manifest your ideas, visions and dreams.

So, think about one of the seeds you want to sow and start dreaming about it unfolding in the most fantastic and spectacular way! It doesn't matter how far-fetched or unrealistic you make this dream. The idea is that you stretch the boundaries of your imagination with this exercise.

For example: You want to set up a healing space, but you need someone to back you financially. Flick the wand and that someone is there! This person loves your ideas and gives you all the money you require to get started. You've begun! You need wonderful therapists to work there with you. No problem! A brilliant receptionist. Hey Presto! An incredible business and marketing manager. Ping! Loads of clients. *Abracadabra!* And so on.

Let the dream take over and explode into a kaleidoscope of countless fantastic, mind-boggling developments...let it become as far-fetched as you like! In fact the more fanciful you are, the better it is. Don't hold back! Don't censor anything! You're just dreaming and giving rein to your creativity. You can do this with anything but just remember to make sure what you want to envisage is not only for your greater good, but for the good of all concerned.

If you come up with any reservations or blocks about doing this, *tap on them*, and rid yourself of a few more limitations. Enjoy the exercise and practise it often. It releases endorphins and it's a lot of fun. Above all, it's a really good way of learning how to loosen yourself from the constraints of self-imposed limitations.

Exercise 41 is adapted from an endorphin exercise by William Bloom.

Welcome Spring

Here's a few more things to do in Spring:

Spring cleaning: When you clean and clear your home you're already having an impact on any negative energy in your environment.

Re-read Chapter 9—Clutter Clearing: Consider what a difference you could make by doing this exercise as it will give you extra impetus for commencing any new plans and projects you may have.

Healing and massage: Go to a Reiki practitioner for some sessions to help get your energies re-balanced. Or, treat yourself to a few massages to ease out any joint or muscle pain that have crept up over the winter months.

Welcome Spring: The official date for the commencement of Spring in the northern hemisphere is on or around March 21st (it's a date that alters slightly according to astronomical calculations, so you need to check it out on the Net for the current year). This date is marked by what is known as the Vernal Equinox. The word Equinox comes from two Latin words: *aequi* (meaning equal) and *nox* (meaning night). It's a time when the sun crosses the equator and causes day and night to be of almost equal length. The ancient Celts used this occurrence as a special marker in their calendar because it signalled the arrival of Spring and rituals were performed for the invocation of fertility, new life, and the planting of new crops

You might like to do Exercise 42, which is a ritual that will help you to manifest the seeds you're planting in Spring.

Exercise 42: Celebration of the Spring Equinox

Buy yourself a couple of packets of herb seeds like parsley and mint which you can grow on a window sill. (It's always useful to have some herbs to hand for cooking and flavouring.) Also, buy yourself a small bag of potting compost and find two small flower pots with saucers for them to stand in. Put some compost in each flower pot and water it so it's moist and ready to receive the seeds when you plant them.

Create a little altar and if you have a piece of green cloth, spread this as a covering over the altar. (Remember, green is the colour of spring!) Decorate your altar with flowers and candles and anything else which seems appropriate.

You might also like to prepare a special meal to eat after the ritual is completed for yourself (and any others who are taking part).

Place the plant pots on the altar. Close the curtains to shut out the light and spend about 15 minutes meditating on the darkness of winter and how spring is bringing the return of the light. Get a sense of that light growing within. Allow the light to fill you and imagine it lifting you up out of the darkness.

Open your eyes and light several candles to symbolise the return of the light.

Then slit open the seed packets and, very solemnly and with great intent, scatter a small amount of parsley seeds in one pot and a small amount of mint seeds in the other, and gently press them into the soil. As you do this, place a hand on each pot and make an affirmation that these seeds symbolise all the seeds you want to plant in your life right now. Spend a few moments thinking about the projects and ideas which are brewing in your mind.

Then water them and as you do so, say out loud words to the effect of:

"I promise to water the seeds I have planted and to nourish them as they grow."

Then place the pots on a window sill where the sun can get to them and watch for the first green shoots.

Every time you look at them, let them be a reminder of what it is you're seeking to grow within yourself.

Feel free to be creative with the ritual and make changes which feel right for you; just make sure that all changes keep to the general theme.

May all your seeds grow and flourish!

Chapter 15

Fire and Abundance

Our ancestors heralded the coming of summer by celebrating the fire festival of Beltane. These festivities were performed in honour of Bel, the Celtic god of light, and took place in the middle of spring when the sun was midpoint in the sky, halfway between the date of the Vernal Equinox (around March 21st) and the Summer Solstice (around June 21st). Fire played an important part in ancient summer rituals because of its kinship to the sun and its symbolism of purification. So at Beltane, bonfires were built to cleanse and rejuvenate the land and its people, and rituals were performed to ensure the sun's life-giving beams would continue to shine down and encourage the fertility of the earth.

Summer

The ancient Celts understood that the sun was crucial for the continuation of life. It melted the ice and brought fresh water gushing forth. It warmed the soil, energised the seeds, ripened the produce and provided them with the food they needed to survive through the coming months. Anticipation was high in expectation of the abundance that summer would bring.

These days, we look forward to the growing heat of the sun for different reasons. Summer conjures thoughts of *al fresco* dining, of outdoor activities like swimming, surfing, sailing and sunbathing, of holidays and cool drinks by the pool and gentle breezes on warm summer nights. Nowadays we celebrate summer as a season of relaxation and play and we spend more time outdoors during both the day and the night than at any other time of the year.

Exercise 43 is a lovely EmoTrance exercise to help you open up to the energising and healing vibrations of Nature and the Earth at the beginning and end of each day.

Exercise 43: Greeting the Day, Greeting the Night

Greeting the Day

Go outside (if you can) as soon as possible after waking. You don't have to be in nature. You can stand outside in the street, or just stick your head out of a window if needs be. It doesn't matter if it's raining or whether the sun is out or not. Just get yourself outside.

Now, take a big breath in and say,

"Day, I greet you!"

Hold in your mind the intention of opening yourself up to the qualities of the day, knowing that you're feeling the unique energies of Nature. Allow yourself to receive these energies into your subtle energy system and to move through you.

Be mindful of any physical responses you may have as you're doing this. Be aware of any emotions arising. If anything comes up for you, notice where you feel it in your body. Place your hands there and stroke and soften the area. Keep doing this until your feelings of discomfort or any sense of rejecting the day have dissipated. Imagine the energy of day moving through you like a river and allow it to flow right through you and out again. Keep allowing this for as long as you like.

Repeat the words: "Day I greet you!" and stay with this openness for a moment or two longer, thanking the day for the lessons and special energies you've received. Then go back into your home and continue with your daily life.

Greeting the Night

Go outside once night has fallen. Breathe in its atmosphere and allow that to help you become more centred and still inside.

Now take a big breath and say,

"Night, I greet you!"

Notice any areas where this makes you feel uncomfortable. Put your hands on this place and soften and flow the energy until it runs smoothly. Be particularly aware of any stuck energies which may have accumulated during the day. As the night flows through you, allow it to wash away tension and stress until any discomfort has dissolved. Let the night take away whatever you no longer need and absorb it into itself.

Thank the night very sincerely for its help and assistance and any lessons it may have given you, then return indoors and continue with your evening activities.

Absorbing the energies of the day and night in this way is very healing, soothing, balancing and energizing. You may notice after doing this even just a few times, that your ability to drink in the day and release whatever energies you don't want or need to the night is easier and that your own energy is feeling clearer. If you can do this exercise every day for a week, you'll really start noticing the difference, and be much more in tune with the wonderful, supportive energies of Nature!

Exercise 43 is an EmoTrance exercise by Silvia Hartmann.

Summer Energies

In summer we tend to focus a great deal on the sun and there are two aspects to its power. On the one hand, there are the positive qualities—purification, cleansing, revitalising and energizing. And on the other hand, there are all the destructive qualities—the fierce heat that cause the rivers to dry, the earth to become parched and barren and the brittle grasses to become vulnerable to bush and forest fires. And let's not forget that with the increase in global warming, we also have to face the dangers of the sun's rays to our skin.

So how can we tune into this paradox and use it to help ourselves?

Well, naturally we need to look at it from an energetic point of view! In the Five Element System of Chinese Medicine, the element of fire equates with the sun and characterises summer. Fire is associated with certain "fiery" qualities like creativity, intuition and enthusiasm, as well as with the emotions of joy and sadness. Fire also governs the heart and the small intestine as well as the Circulation–Sex Meridian (which protects the heart) and the Triple Warmer Meridian (which governs our flight or fight responses.)

We can therefore see that this element powerfully affects not only our main life support system (the heart), but also our digestion. And from an energetic level, we can interpret the word "digestion" to mean how we deal with our feelings and emotions, how we cope with the words, actions and deeds of others, and how we manage successes and setbacks. Any degree of discomfort around these issues can be seen as an energetic form of indigestion that will affect us whether we're conscious of it or not. It's likely to manifest in emotions like anger, hurt, resentment and frustration, etc. Add this to the widespread 21st century malaise of stress, and we can see that the fire element literally sparks off all manner of responses, from encouraging a healthy vitality, intellect and creativity, to causing us to overwork, become performance-driven and deeply stressed.

Stress Signals

Bearing all this in mind, one of the first things the arrival of summer can remind you to do is to check out where you are with your stress levels! You've seen from previous chapters how detrimental stress can be in terms of our health and well-being and how we need to be constantly alert to it creeping up on us. If we don't keep an eye on it and try to nip any symptoms in the bud, it can lead to burn-out and exhaustion as well as health problems like high blood pressure and heart disease.

Here's a short list of some of the warning signs of stress to watch out for:

- Your concentration is poor and you tend not to think straight.
- Your body is seized up with tension especially across the shoulders and neck.
- You may suffer from stomach upsets.
- You don't sleep well or you can't sleep.
- You're in a constant state of nervousness.

Below is a reminder of some of the things you've already learnt about in this book and a few extra suggestions which can help you to either avoid or alleviate stress:

- Have a look back at Exercise 10 (page 33), Exercise 11 (page 35), and Exercise 12 (page 36) to try some of the pacing techniques.

- Laughter is amazing medicine. It relaxes you, helps you to come out of yourself and be more spontaneous, boosts the immune system and triggers endorphins. Actively seek out entertainment which makes you laugh; e.g., funny films, TV shows or books. Laughter is a wonderful antidote to stress and can help you to lighten up.

- Re-read Chapter 6 and think about setting up a meditation practise if you haven't already done so. Try Exercise 16 (page 47), the Walking Meditation, if you find it hard to sit still with the eyes closed.

- A good phrase to write out and stick up on your wall somewhere as a reminder not to wind yourself up is: Worry is like a rocking chair—it keeps you occupied but it doesn't get you anywhere!

- Seek professional help if you need it.

Burnout Signs

Lots of people think that "burnout" is just another name for being stressed, but it's not, and it's important to understand the difference between the two syndromes. First of all, people who are suffering from stress usually *know* that they're under too much pressure mentally, physically and emotionally and they're able to acknowledge this, even if they don't do anything about it! However, people suffering from burnout tend not to know when it's happening. This is because they're typically too overcome with feeling as though they're being buried under a mountain of difficulty, struggle and increasing helplessness and hopelessness.

Warning signs of burnout

- Every day there's always too much to do.
- No time to wind down or relax properly.
- Your immune system is weakened and you're constantly getting viruses, fighting off bugs or feeling below par.
- You're filled with self doubt and a sense of failure.
- You're feeling tired or drained most of the time.
- You're suffering from frequent muscle and backaches as well as headaches.

- You feel empty and devoid of motivation.
- Everything feels like a waste of time.
- You feel overwhelmed, overloaded and depressed.

If preventative action is taken when still in the "stressed" mode, this should help you to avoid burnout. Once in burnout, however, the first thing to do is to be able to accept that you're there and decide to do something about it.

An obvious first resource would be to try EFT, using the Basic Recipe as explained in Chapter 13.

You could also add in any or all of the following:

- Use Exercise 2 (page 5), Creating a Safe Place, and go to sleep in it.
- Try the Blue Mist exercise (Exercise 13, page 37).
- Build some regular exercise into your weekly schedule, like going to a Yoga or Tai Chi Class, that will also help you relax and centre yourself. This kind of exercise will also help you to sleep better.
- Book yourself some massage or, better still, some Reiki sessions to give you some deep energy healing. At some point, you might like to consider learning the first level of Reiki and then you'll be able to give yourself regular self-healing at any time or place.
- If it all feels too much, seek help and support from a professional therapist.

Of course, stress isn't something that happens only in the summer. It can happen at any time of the year. There's no use relying on holidays to get you out of stress. That's just a temporary solution. If you're prone to stress, you need to keep a watchful eye on it and work consistently with techniques which help you to relax and find greater peace of mind. And summer is a great time of year to do some maintenance work!

Loving Oneself

The element of fire also relates to sexual energy and creative potential. This chimes harmoniously with old traditions linking Midsummer with passion, love and romance. The June moon became known as the Honey Moon because of the proliferation of honey in the hives, and June has long been well known as a popular month for weddings.

So if summer is stirring your sexual passion and you find yourself wishing to attract a new partner into your life, the first thing to do is to take a good, long look at how you feel about yourself. Why? *Because the most important relationship you'll ever have with anyone is with yourself!*

Remember: thoughts are energy, so if you don't like yourself in some way or another, you're sending out negative vibrations which can put people off on a very subtle level. Think of what the hormones adrenaline and cortisol are doing to you if you're constantly criticising yourself.

Feeling good about yourself makes you very attractive to others!

It's really important to be aware of any critical, judgemental, or uncaring feelings towards yourself. If you have a negative attitude you're not only cutting yourself off from your connection to your own vital energy but also to the energies around you. You're blocking the flow of the Chi! When you do that, you're creating difficulties for yourself on both an inner and outer level.

Learning to apply love, care and nurture towards yourself is vital for your well-being. Developing love and compassion towards yourself is part and parcel of finding the path that leads to a healthy relationship. As Rumi, the great 13th century Persian poet and mystic, said, "Your task is not to seek love, but merely to seek and find all the barriers within yourself which you have built against it."

The books by Louise Hay are a wonderful first resource for starting to look at oneself in a more loving and understanding manner. Many, many books have been written on the problems arising about our relationships with ourselves and others, and I've included some authors and titles in the Further Information and Suggested Reading section at the back of the book. In addition, I highly recommend Sandra Hilawi's EmoTrance workbook on healing and transforming your love life.

The Growth of Summer

There's a lot of flowering and flourishing going on as the sun grows stronger, and it's important to see how we're ripening and blossoming along with everything else. Summer is the time when we can start to see the fruits of the seeds we planted back in the Spring.

Exercise 44 will help you determine how your inner "garden" is coming along?

Exercise 44: Counting the Buds and the Blossoms

Take a look at what personal seeds you planted in the Spring.

- Are there any which haven't yet sprouted green shoots and shown their heads above the soil?
- What seeds are growing strongly?
- What seeds need some added TLC to help them on their way?
- What seeds are providing you with new views and attitudes?
- Which ones are bringing about fresh ideas and opportunities?

Make a list of everything you can see that is now growing—even those things which may have grown only a little.

By keeping an eye on what's beginning to flourish you start to become more aware of what's happening within you so little by little your growth becomes more conscious.

Don't start beating yourself up about things which haven't sprouted. You're in the process of making changes within yourself and you can't do everything at once.

Where we fall by the wayside with one thing we may be establishing something very positive and beneficial in another.

Give yourself some appreciation for what you've done. If you can see that some bad habits are creeping back or growing of their own accord, you can do a bit of weeding!

You've got plenty of aids and techniques to choose from now.

Ask yourself: what could I do to help me with (whatever)?

And then do it

Helpful Things to Do in Summer

Do pleasurable things: Go back to Exercise 6 (page 21), Working with the Best Things in Your Life. Remind yourself about which things were really enjoyable and easily done and make a promise to yourself to do at least *one* of these every week.

Get some fresh air and sunlight each day: Even if the sun isn't shining, you can still benefit from the light that will help to energise the mind. The fresh air will also clear the cobwebs and be better for your breathing.

Spend time with children if possible: This is a great way of loosening up and re-discovering your own sense of play and spontaneity. Children have so much energy and are able to thrill to simple things like running around on the grass barefoot, building sand castles on the beach, or creating games. Join in the fun and make contact with the child that still lives within you.

Do some Journaling: If you haven't already started keeping a journal, try to make summer the time to start. It's a wonderful way of becoming more aware of the growing that's taking place within. With every encounter and experience, with every thought, with every understanding, we grow. The more we gain a sense of clarity about what's happening to us, and where we are, the better we can see what we can do to help ourselves to find our personal rivers.

Abundance Thinking

Summer is a time of in-your-face abundance as nature bursts into a riot of vegetation and colour. We can sense abundance on an inner level, too. This feeling arises when you're flowing and growing without any sense of struggle or effort to make it happen. We experience abundance when we have a deep feeling of stillness or when we feel the fullness of an expansive heart. We feel abundance when we're at peace and wanting nothing.

You see, abundance doesn't have to be about riches or wealth or possessions. It can often come most powerfully from the really simple things in life—most of which cost you absolutely *nothing* to have! That holiday feeling of time off from the grind of work can give you a sense of abundance, as can lying by the sea listening to the waves lapping at the shore. It can come from the warmth and love of being amongst good, dear friends or family, from receiving a sudden and unexpected smile, from being with your lover, or hearing the rain lashing against the window whilst you lie in bed, safe and warm and secure.

We live in an abundant Universe. The Earth, Nature, and the Cosmos are all filled with beautiful, benevolent wave fields. Tuning into them generates a sense of peace, calm, wonder and awe. And when we experience this feeling it's because we're 100% present in the moment. We're not worrying about the future or the past. We're just being present with what's happening and where we are right now. We are *being*, not *doing*. Someone once said it was good to remember that we're human beings not human doings! Present moment awareness is the best state to be in, because it keeps us in the *now* and makes us feel more grounded and centred.

It's really important to acknowledge where we find abundance in every area of our lives and to develop a sense of gratitude for what we have instead of only dwelling on what we don't have. This will remind you of the positive things in life, and by placing your focus in this direction, you're more likely to attract further good things. This is what the Law of Attraction is all about. Basically, it's saying that because we're electro-magnetic creatures, we naturally attract things to us according to the vibrations we exude. "You are the creator of your own experience whether you know that you are or not. Your life experience is unfolding in precise response to the vibrations which radiate as a result of your thoughts, whether you know that it is or not."*

The mind is very powerful. Remember: as we think, so we create. Therefore, if you spend most of your time focussing on the negative, criticising and judging yourself and others, constantly imagining worst case scenarios, always believing or expecting the worst of people—guess what? You'll attract even more of those things into your life! Thoughts are magnetic. So watch your thoughts! Start becoming aware of how many times each day negativity

---

* From *Ask and It is Given*, by Esther and Jerry Hicks.

is running through your mind and actively seek to change that by replacing negative thoughts with positive ones.

Developing an attitude of gratitude for all the things you have rather than focussing on all the things you lack is the best way of fostering abundance in your life. So start training yourself to say thank you for everything. Yes, everything! Open yourself up to the possibility of understanding that all things and situations—even the most difficult ones—can be learning situations and be grateful for that. Remember, there's always a purpose to a problem or an obstacle if you look for it. If you start thinking in this way, you can change your attitude towards challenges and setbacks and this automatically helps you to see them in a different light. You can then begin to deal with them in more skilful ways. Train yourself out of dreaming up negative scenarios! Think positively and you can change your whole world. (There's loads of information on the subject of abundance in the Further Information and Suggested Reading section at the back of the book.)

Celebrate Summer

Summer's a great time for celebrating your achievements and successes and the best occasion to do this is on the day of the Summer Solstice.

What is the Summer Solstice?

Well, during the spring and summer months the noonday sun, quite visibly, has been climbing higher and higher in the sky on each successive day. But there comes a point, on or around June 21st, when it moves imperceptibly and gives the impression of standing still in the sky. This is the day of the Summer Solstice that causes the longest day and the shortest night of the year. (The word solstice comes from two Latin words: *sol*, which means sun, and *sistere*, which means to stand still.) After the Summer Solstice, the sun immediately begins to wane. The journey towards autumn and harvest has begun and the days will slowly begin to shorten.

The Festival of Midsummer is another Fire Festival. It represents a high point of the year and a time when a great deal of powerful energy is all around us. Many ancient buildings were aligned to the exact spot where the sun rises on the day of the Summer Solstice (the main entrance at Stonehenge is a good example of this). This was done in order to catch some of the sun's power and fill places of worship with its energy. Traditionally celebrations on this day included the kindling of fires from the wood of oak and fir and throwing herbs into the flames. The herbs were purifying and reviving and said to drive away disease. People would feast and dance and jump over the flames of the fire for luck and fertility.

If you'd like to celebrate the Summer Solstice in your own way, Exercise 45 (page 154) can serve as an example of how to do this. (Feel free to add in your own ideas about what this ritual should include.) You can, of course, celebrate it on your own, but it's always more fun—if you've got some like-minded friends—to throw a Summer Solstice party and invite them to join in with the ritual. You could ask everyone to bring some food and something to drink so that all present will have contributed to the celebration.

Exercise 45: Summer Solstice—Celebrating Your Achievements

Check the date of the Summer Solstice as it varies from year to year

The night before, (Midsummer's Eve) spend some time making a list of all your achievements this year, no matter how big or how small. Write them on a clean piece of paper, roll it up into a scroll and tie it with a ribbon or a piece of string. If you're planning on a party, suggest to your friends who are coming that they do the same and bring their scrolls with them. Make it clear that the lists are private and don't have to be read out—unless someone particularly wants to do so.

Make an altar and this time spread it with some yellow fabric—if you have it—for yellow is the colour of summer. Add flowers and candles and any other things which have meaning for you.

If you've got friends coming, ask them all to bring a candle or two in holders as well. These can be placed on the altar and other (safe) areas in the room so that when it comes to lighting them all, you've literally got a bank of candles burning which will look wonderful and symbolise the power of the sun.

If you have a garden, gather some flowers from there and weave them into a summer wreath. You can easily make this by bending a wire coat hanger into a circle and then winding some ivy around it to give a base through which you can weave in some flowers and herbs. If you don't have a garden, don't worry. A vase of flowers will do. Ask your friends if they would like to bring flowers and wreaths as well. Explain that flowers gathered from their own gardens, or picked from hedgerows and nature can be used symbolically to represent personal achievements and successes.

Set out the food and drink ready for the feasting afterwards and maybe put on some joyful music.

Place your wreath or flowers on your altar as well as your scroll of achievements. Invite any friends who are coming to do the same as and when they arrive.

When you're ready to start, light the candles and as you do so, think about your achievements and give yourself some appreciation for your efforts.

Then find a place to sit down quietly and start meditating on abundance. Bring to mind all the things which help you to feel this way and let those feelings fill you to the brim.

After about 15 to 20 minutes, gently come out of the meditation. Place a fireproof bowl on the floor in the centre of the room together with a jug of water and one of the candles. Take your scroll of achievements and ceremoniously burn it, allowing it to turn to ashes in the fireproof bowl. (The jug of water is there to act as a fire extinguisher in case you need it!) Invite your friends to do the same if you've got some people with you.

You could throw some lavender or verbena into the bowl as the scrolls burn to symbolise purification and revitalisation. Later you could scatter the ashes outside your home or in your garden to evoke powers of protection and good fortune.

Afterwards, pour out a drink and toast the Summer. Then get into the music and start dancing. Enjoy the movement of your body as you swing and sway. Clap your hands, swing your arms, shake your head and flex your feet. Dancing moves your energies and opens up the channels. It's endorphinating and it's very beneficial!

Enjoy the party!

If we can reach out to nature and feel its vibrancy, we can strengthen and harmonise our energy systems so that we can function at more optimum levels, open our hearts to the all the summer vibrations and allow them to help us in whatever ways we need.

Above all, remember that summer is a celebration of life!

Appreciate your gifts
Celebrate your Achievements
And bless the Earth

Chapter 16

Harvest and Light

Summer draws to a final close with the advent of the Autumn Equinox around the 22nd or 23rd September. Almost imperceptibly, the days begin getting shorter and the nights gradually cooler from the moment we pass the Summer Solstice. By the Autumn Equinox, Nature has begun to withdraw her energies and turn inwards for a period of rest and reflection in the coming months.

Autumn

Autumn is the time for harvesting the crops which were planted in Spring and Harvest Festivals are celebrated all over the world by many different cultures with songs and prayers of gratitude for the fruits of the earth. In the old Celtic religion, gifts were offered and sacrifices made over a course of three different Harvest Festivals. These were: Lammas for the harvest of grain on August 1st, Mabon at the time of the Autumn Equinox in September for the harvest of fruit, and Samhain (pronounced Sow'in and meaning Summer's End), on October 31st, for the harvest of meat.

Aside from the Harvest, our distant ancestors recognised the dying back of the leaves, flowers and plants as a time to remember the dead. Samhain, therefore, became an important time for honouring the ancestors. On that night, the Gods of the Otherworlds and the spirits of the dead were believed to mingle with men. In later years, as Christianity spread, the old traditions were suppressed and transformed into more acceptable Christian ones. This is how Samhain eventually became Halloween which, as we all know, is the night when ghouls and ghosties are supposed to walk the earth!

It's easy to see the relevance of Harvest Festivals to our personal growth. Reaping your very own harvest is about remembering your connection to the planet and your physical need for nutrition. It's about looking to see what you've learnt and understood and the knowledge you've gathered over the past months. And it's also about celebrating that sense of completion that comes when anything you planted consciously in Spring has come into being; e.g., a desired goal, a problem overcome, new attitudes or more skilful coping mechanisms. Above all, it's about feeling a sense of gratitude for the things which you have and the blessings you've received.

Developing Gratitude

I touched on the subject of gratitude briefly in the last chapter, but it's such a relevant subject for Autumn, I want tell you more about how it can help you make real transformations in your life.

Scientific research has shown that practising the attitude of gratitude can raise your happiness "set-point". A new field of psychology called Positive Psychology came into being in 1998 through the work of American Psychologist Martin Seligman, who researched what effects feeling good could have on people. He discovered that relationships and friendships were better, that people were more focussed, more creative and had a higher productivity, and that happy people coped better when things got bad. He also found that positive thoughts can undo the harmful effects that negative emotions can have on our state of well-being. (Believe me—you can't feel gratitude when you're feeling negative!) But most importantly, it was found that gratitude is the best way of raising happiness levels.

It's really helpful if you can learn to accept things the way they are. This doesn't mean that you're going to become a doormat and be walked over or allow yourself to get mowed down by difficulties, you're simply accepting that this is how it is *at this moment in time*. You can learn from every situation—good or bad—so it's good to be grateful for that. It's also important to accept your share of responsibility for what's happening in your life without either beating yourself up or going into denial. It helps to remember that if you're partly responsible for any currently undesirable situation in your life, you're also capable of transforming it into something more positive. The good news is, *whatever* caused your problems, you now have techniques to transform them! And you can be very grateful for that!!

It's important also to remember to express gratitude verbally and not just think about it. The 13th-century German philosopher and theologian, Meister Eckhart said, "If the only prayer you said in your whole life was 'thank you,' that would suffice." Remembering to thank everybody for both the large and the small acts of kindness and consideration you receive fosters good relationships and better communication. And it helps you to stop taking people for granted—which nobody likes. Folk will always respond well to appreciation for something they've done or said. It makes them happy, and it's very good to spread some happiness around! Giving to others what you seek for yourself is a great way of bringing more of that thing into your life.

As you learn to develop and maintain a sense of gratitude for everything, so your whole energy system begins vibrating at a higher frequency. If you think this sounds flaky, remember how much your thoughts can affect the chemistry of your body, and the even flow of your subtle energy! You're essentially an electromagnetic being, so this means that when your energy vibrations are raised, you naturally begin to resonate and align yourself with the higher vibrations humming in the Universe. So, if you're constantly "transmitting" positive vibes and thoughts, you're automatically able to attract and receive more beneficial events and circumstances into your life.

I've personally worked to eradicate an awful lot of negativity from my life and can promise you that practising gratitude can be enormously transforming and beneficial. So why not give it a try and spend a bit of time and energy getting into the habit of it?

Exercise 46 can help you to bring more gratitude into your everyday life:

Exercise 46: Gratitude Lists

Gratitude is a reminder that the small things in life are often the most precious. Appreciating these things makes it easier to change pessimistic attitudes towards challenges and setbacks.

- As you go through each day, make a note of anything that might have happened for which you feel gratitude. It might have been finding a seat on the train to work instead of having to stand all the way, a welcome phone call or email from a friend, feeling grateful that the sun was shining, a little bit of kindness or understanding from a work colleague, or delighting in the sight of some pretty flowers in somebody's front garden. The more you think in terms of gratitude, abundance of every kind is drawn towards you.
- Keep a notebook and a pen beside your bed, and before you go to sleep each night, write down *five* things which have happened during the day and for which you are grateful.

Beside each of the five things, write a few words about how they've benefitted you.

Once gratitude lists become easier to compile, you can start making mental ones instead at bedtime. I find that mentally going through the day and feeling gratitude for the smallest things which have happened is a great way of falling asleep. It takes you into a more positive frame of mind and frequently results in feeling better about yourself and the world when you wake up.

Other things you could do to help you feel gratitude:

- Practise the Inner Smile guided meditation (Exercise 5, page 13). It's an easy way to send gratitude to your body and any endorphinating exercise is good for your health!
- Take better care of your body. It's done a really good job of carrying you around from A to B all this time and deserves some TLC and appreciation! Check back through Chapter 3, Body Basics.

- If you wake up in the middle of the night with your mind churning over various things that are causing you anxiety, switch modes and start thinking of all the things you appreciate in your life instead.

Balancing Your Life

The Autumn Equinox is a time when the lengths of night and day are more or less equal, and we can use this as a reminder to bring more balance into our lives. All our daily activities—such as going to work, relaxing, socialising, having relationships or spending time in quiet contemplation—take up most of the waking day and it's important to ensure that some of these activities don't exclude the existence of others. Now is therefore a good time to check out where you might need to re-balance things in your life.

Exercise 47 is a very simple way of bringing balance into your life by drawing what is known as a "Life Pie".

Exercise 47: Drawing a Life Pie

Take a clean piece of paper and on it draw a circle of about 2 to 3 inches in diameter. This is your "pie". Then look at the following headings which are the main areas of focus and activity for the average person:

- Work
- Family
- Play
- Romance
- Exercise
- Adventure (i.e., new activities)
- Friends/Social Life
- Spirituality

Using these headings, allocate a segment of your pie to each of them, but make each segment proportional to the amount of focus you give to each area. You'll almost certainly discover that your "portions" will be of varying sizes. For example, "work" might be a very large portion and "play" might be very small.

This gives you a very graphic overview of which areas of your life are taking up most space and where you may need to find ways of balancing things up.

Look to see what you might do to let go of particular things that are causing an imbalance in your life.

Coping With Change

As the trees become bare and the evenings become darker, we have to face the fact that all things must pass. Nature reveals endless sequences of change and Autumn expresses this very clearly. It's very much a time of transition which often brings up a sense of impending loss and melancholy in people.

But life is about change! Nothing ever stays the same. We're born, we grow, we live and we die. Everything goes through this cycle—the fruit, the vegetables, the crops, the animals, the birds and the fish. Even mountains and rocks are subject to change, for they too grow, erode and decay. There are also mini-cycles of birthing and dying within each of our lives. We see this in the ending of relationships and other attachments, in things that manifest into our lives only to disappear once again, and in the way the physical body changes over time.

Change is the only constant in life. Nothing grows without going through changes.

Wanting to change is the first step towards making that change. But, if you've found in the past that your attempts at change have often come to naught, it usually means there's some deep resistance inside you that is preventing it. In order to make change, we need to find ways of letting go of the things that hold us back.

Before we proceed any further, let me reassure you that it's OK to be anxious about making changes! It's a perfectly normal human reaction. So you're not weak or hopeless or useless if you feel this way.

Resistance to change is frequently linked to fear, which is often about not feeling safe. And if you don't feel safe about doing something, no matter how much you (or other people) say you've got to do it, you're unlikely to take any action towards trying to alter the situation. There may also be a nagging uncertainty that even if you can make this change, things aren't necessarily going to be any better. You might even be afraid that you're not going to be able to cope with any changes after you've made them.

Sometimes people find themselves in two minds about wanting to change. A part of you wants to and another part of you doesn't. This brings stalemate. No movement and no change. It's also possible to become so firmly attached to problems, that they become a protection against having to do anything about them! Again, you stay stuck.

If feeling unsafe is a big factor in you not making a much-needed or desired change, it's incredibly important to find a way through that fear before you attempt to make any changes at all!

So how can you help yourself in that situation?

Well, remember that any resistance or anxiety you feel around the idea of making changes is going to be lodged somewhere in your body. So energy work is clearly indicated and my suggestion is to use EmoTrance in the first instance. It's such a gentle way of shifting energy and always allows you to work at your own pace. This is important because you need to be very kind to yourself when trying to open up to the possibility of change, particularly if you've been stuck in this area for some time. If you can accept that safety issues are preventing you from letting go and moving on, and you're willing to work slowly and carefully on that, then you can begin.

Exercise 48 will help you gain skill in making changes. Notice that you're not trying to make any specific change, you're just moving towards a point where it feels less scary to even contemplate making a change.

Exercise 48: Approaching Change

Ask yourself, "When I think about how unsafe it feels to change, where do I feel that in my body?"

Put your hands on your body exactly where you feel this energy of "unsafe-ness". Ask yourself where this energy wants to flow. Encourage it to move by stroking it in its chosen direction. Soften and flow and allow it to move.

Keep going till it feels as though it's gone.

Take a big breath and then go back inside your body to check whether you feel more at ease with the idea of making some change(s).

If there's still a feeling in your body around that anxiety, where do you feel it? Take yourself through the EmoTrance process again until you feel more at ease with the idea of going into this at a deeper level.

It's unrealistic at this stage to imagine that you can let go of *all* your anxiety about change. But, if you can get to a point where it's subsided enough for you to feel a lot *safer*, then it's OK to proceed further—if you feel ready.

Once you're feeling safer about the idea of change you could then try shifting into another gear with this way of working. Let's suppose, for example, that you're thinking of selling up (or leaving) where you live at the moment and moving out to a particular place in the country. You could now begin to explore some of the feelings and emotions which are underlying that fear. Try completing the statements below:

- The downside to making these changes is _____ (by "downside", I mean how might making this change cause you further problems?)

- Thinking about making these changes reminds me of ____ .

- Rather than making these changes, what I really want is ____ .

- I'd be more willing to make these changes if ____ .

This should give you some clarity on what's going on for you beneath the surface.

You could also explore anything that came up when you completed these statements by using a mixture of EmoTrance and EFT. (Both these techniques work seamlessly together and are an amazingly good combination to use when relevant.) Exercise 49 guides you through how to do this.

Exercise 49: Making Changes Using EmoTrance and/or EFT

Suppose the thought of moving to the country brings up painful childhood memories of leaving your familiar home and moving to a strange place that felt lonely and uncomfortable. Identify where you feel the pain of this memory in your body and EmoTrance it.

If you should find the energy doesn't move, you may need to be more focused on precisely what's coming up for you, in which case, you should try using EFT on it as follows:

First, calibrate the intensity

Example Setup: "Even though the thought of making this move reminds me of _____, I deeply and completely accept myself" (say this three times while tapping on the KC).

Example Reminder Phrase: "It reminds me of _____ "(tapping twice through all the other points in the EFT sequence)

Breathe and re-calibrate

Keep going through the Setups and Rounds till you've got to zero

If any other aspects around this issue come up, work through each of them until you get the intensity down to zero. To help you really nail the core of the problem, you might find it useful to ask yourself the following questions and use EFT or EmoTrance on what comes to mind:

- Who might be jealous or upset if I make this change?
- What will people expect of me if I make this change?
- What will I do if this change doesn't make things any better?

Remember: If you can't shift stuff with EmoTrance, then switch to EFT.

As you can see, dealing with resistance and making changes needs to be approached with great care and patience and a willingness to spend as much time on this as you need. However, if you find it's too difficult to handle on your own, do seek out a qualified EmoTrance or EFT practitioner in your area to help you. Remember that Energy Therapy doesn't tie you up for weeks, months and years but can help you to make effective positive shifts, often very quickly. You may only need a few sessions to get you over the initial difficulties and then find you're able to continue doing further work on your own.

Additional insights about the situation may arise from journaling and writing out how you're feeling, so you could also use a combination of this with EFT and EmoTrance.

Autumn Traditions

There are many things that can help you prepare for Autumn, but here are two I've found very helpful:

- **Clear out clutter:** letting go of stuff you don't need on an outer level encourages the same process on an inner one (Chapter 9).

- **Do some Space Clearing:** it creates supportive energies in your home to help with any transition (see Chapter 10).

For the ancient Celts, the drawing in of the autumnal nights brought to mind the forces of darkness and the evils of men. This caused them to begin focusing more on the Light as an antidote and a reminder that good can triumph over evil. They wove these concepts into rituals and revelry and this gave birth to the many Festivals of Light which are celebrated at this time of year. These festivals are still observed today in many different cultures around the world making this period a truly magical time, full of intensely building spiritual vibrations which continue throughout Autumn and into Winter.

A Festival of Light is about cleansing and washing away the sins and misdeeds of mankind. It's also about banishing evil, starting afresh, rejoicing in the family, appreciating friendships, and, often, about the giving and receiving of gifts. The most well known of the Light Festivals is of course the Christian tradition of Christmas, with all its emphasis on lights (cleansing) and bells (clearing), the giving of gifts and, of course, not forgetting the birth of the Christian Saviour of Mankind, Jesus Christ. Other notable Light Festivals include Diwali (sometimes known as the Hindu Christmas) where people light candles and lamps to symbolise the victory of light over darkness. There's also a Jewish Festival of Lights called Hanukah where the lamps which are lit symbolise good overcoming evil.

All the major religions traditionally use candles and lamps as symbols to represent their spirit or soul being cleansed and purified and you'll find that Light is used in this context in temples, mosques and churches all over the world. Candles are lit for invocations and worship. Light is also used to signify the summoning of higher energies and as such is very powerful.

Exercise 50 is a lovely meditation I learnt many years ago that invokes the spirit of Light and is an excellent way of cleansing your Chakras or energy centres.

Exercise 50: The Flame

Sit in a comfortable meditation position with your back straight. Close your eyes and come into your breath. Spend time following your breath (Exercise 14, page 44) until the chatter in your mind is quieter.

Then imagine that deep, down inside you at the base of your torso (Base Chakra), a small flame is burning. Imagine it like the small flame given off by a votive candle. There it is, burning and glowing softly, deep down inside of you.

Bring all of your attention to this small flame and visualise it flickering gently with a small aura surrounding it. Now, imagine that as you watch it the flame grows taller, and as it does, the light around it expands and grows larger and wider. Imagine the tip of the flame extending up towards your belly button (Second Chakra), the bright light fills your lower torso and abdomen, your legs, and your feet.

Now, as you gaze upon the flame, it continues to grow taller, and the tip of the flame extends upwards towards your diaphragm area. As it does, the light in your lower torso expands upwards to fill your body to just underneath the breast line (Third Chakra).

And still the flame grows taller. Now the tip of the flame extends up towards your heart (Heart Chakra), and as it does so, the light expands even more and fills your entire chest area.

The whole of your torso is now filled with light.

And the tip of the flame continues to grow, reaching up now towards your throat (Throat Chakra), filling your throat with its light. As it reaches your throat, the light also fills up your arms and your hands.

The flame continues to grow higher. Now it extends up to that place between your eyebrows (Brow Chakra) which is known as the eye centre. As it does, it fills your head with its light.

The flame climbs higher still, now reaching up to the crown of your head (Crown Chakra). When it reaches this point, the light within you expands and stretches out beyond the confines of your body, filtering out into your aura, filling it with light.

Your entire body and aura is now filled with light. You're surrounded by a bubble of healing light. Let the light fill every part of you—your bones, muscles, organs, cells—and bathe in it. Nothing can harm you. All is well.

Enjoy being in this place for as long as you wish.

When you're ready, come back into the room slowly and open your eyes.

Rest a while in the afterglow of this experience.

Autumn Celebration

I can't close this chapter without offering you a ritual for celebrating the Autumn Equinox! Remember to check the date as it changes from year to year. Doing these rituals is very helpful for evoking the energy of the time and complements the work you can do on yourself at each season. (As before, feel free to create your own interpretation of it if you prefer.)

Before doing this ritual, it's particularly important to have prepared some good food for eating afterwards, because it so completely symbolises the sense of Autumnal plenty and abundance. Try to use some seasonal produce in whatever dishes you prepare. This would be another time when you could invite some like-minded friends along to join you and make it more of a celebration. Or do the ritual on your own first and *then* invite good friends—like-minded or not—to come and join you afterwards!

Exercise 51 is my version.

Exercise 51: A Ritual for the Autumnal Equinox

A few days beforehand, start looking for some beautiful natural things to use as offerings for this ritual. You might choose some spectacular autumn leaves or fabulous pine cones, or some interesting pebbles or shells.

The night before the Equinox, spend time journaling about your harvest and making a list of the following:

- All the things you're grateful for.
- All the things you'd like to manifest in your life.
- All the negative things you'd like to release.
- All the areas in your life where you need to achieve a better balance.

On the day of the Equinox, create an altar. Spread your altar with fabric in the autumnal colours of red, orange, gold and brown. If you like, put a joss stick and holder on the altar with your favourite aroma. Perhaps place a vase of flowers there together with red, orange or gold candles, as well as a bowl or basket of autumn produce containing apples, squash, gourds, grapes, pomegranates, and nuts, etc. Add a fine loaf of bread. If you can find them, add some corn dollies.

Place all the things you've chosen for your offering on a small tray together with a glass of wine or cider. Add a few votive candles and scatter some flower heads around the objects. Keep this tray to the side of the altar until you need it.

When you're ready to begin, take off your shoes and light all the candles and the joss sticks, including the votive candles on the tray you've prepared with your offerings.

Pick up the tray and stand with it in front of your altar.

Centre yourself well by connecting to your Hara and breathe into the Hara area (Exercise 32, page 90). This will help you to ground and connect to the Earth. Stay with this for a few moments.

When you're ready, raise the tray of offerings aloft and give thanks out loud for your personal harvest, blessings and abundance. You could say something like:

Dear Mother Earth/Universe/Mother–Father God/Divine Spirit/God
(or use whatever form of address feels right for you),
I give thanks for all the blessings and abundance I've received this year.
I give thanks for all the blessings and abundance which are to come.
Please receive these offerings with all my gratitude and appreciation."

Place the tray of offerings and votive candles on the altar with great reverence. Then sit down to meditate.

As you turn your mind inwards, recall those areas of yourself that don't serve you well (like behaviours or attitudes) and that you'd like to let go of or change. Imagine they're just lots of little pieces of energy which are shaped like leaves. And as you sit there in meditation, visualize them gently releasing themselves from the branches of the trees and falling down to the ground where they'll become compost for the earth and make it a fertile place for new things to grow.

Stay with this image for as long as you wish. Then, when you feel ready, come back, open your eyes and take your time to stand up.

Now, reach for that glass of wine or cider which was on your tray of offerings. If you have a garden, take it outside and pour it on the earth as a final offering. If you don't have a garden, sip it yourself and give thanks once more!

Then enjoy your feast!

Let the Light lift you up!
Wonderful gifts and blessings
to each and every one of you!

Chapter 17

The Return of the Sun

In the old days, winter was thought to commence after Samhain, for this is the time Nature was seen as noticeably retreating within herself and withdrawing her energies. The long nights and the dark mornings reflected this, as did the leafless trees, the lack of vegetation, and the hibernation of certain animals. The ancient Celts understood that the earth needed to sleep in winter in order to regenerate her energies after all her efforts in the previous seasons.

Nature's resting period continues throughout November and late December and during this time, the sun sinks lower and lower on the horizon. Then comes the Winter Solstice, which happens around December 21st or 22nd, and at that point, because of the tilt of the earth's axis, the sun starts climbing higher in the sky.

Winter

Winter Solstice was a very auspicious time for the ancient Celts because they believed the sun had overcome the darkness and was being re-born. This gave rise to great celebrations and feasting in honour of the new-born Solstice Sun. They called this festival "Yule", and their rituals around this occasion included offerings and merry making, as well as burning large "Yule logs" to symbolize the return of the Light.

Yule was celebrated as a time of family gatherings and goodwill towards all people. Sprigs of the sacred mistletoe plant were hung over their doorways to protect them from evil and as a sign of peace and friendship. They also decorated their homes with evergreen branches and stems of holly and ivy. Holly represented the masculine, and the soft, winding stems of ivy signified the feminine. This greenery was used to symbolise the fact that the earth never dies, but merely sleeps, and that the green shoots of new life will come once again in the spring. To this day, we still festoon our homes with holly, ivy and mistletoe over the Festive Season, and many of our Christmas traditions such as merry-making, feasting, generosity, and connection with family and friends are based on these ancient Yule festivities. The use of candles as decorations as well as twinkling strings of fairy lights are also echoes of the fact that Christmas is a Festival of Light.

At Winter Solstice, the people looked forward to the coming of Spring, the return of the Light, and the re-generation of Nature. As it was also an important turning point in the cycle of the sun; this time of year was linked with concepts of birth and death as well as beginnings and endings. January, the first month of the New Year, is named after the Roman God Janus who was always depicted with two heads—one looking backwards and the other forwards. He was honoured as the God of Departure and Return and he was also the God of New Beginnings.

The ancient understandings around Janus are the basis for the traditional practise of making New Year resolutions. But, as I said, my view is that February or March is a better time for resolutions because that's when the energy begins to rise and there's more impetus for actually carrying them out.

Reflection

In terms of how we translate all this into our personal work, we can see immediately that, in winter, Nature is encouraging us to be less active and to take things at a gentler pace. And as the cold weather tends to push us inwards and make us more introspective, so it follows that we need to use this time to enter a period of reflection and *gently* uncover what we need to work upon in the coming year.

Exercise 52 will help you in doing this.

Exercise 52: New Year Reflections

Ask yourself the following questions and write down the answers in a notebook so that you can refer to them in the following year:

- When do I feel that my life is most meaningful?
- What would bring me more happiness than anything else in the world?
- Have I ever told those who mean the most to me how I feel about them?
- Which of my friendships in the last year was the most mutually supportive and why?
- In what ways did I nourish my most intimate relationship last year? (If you don't have a significant other in your life, remember that, in fact, your most intimate relationship is always with yourself!)
- What are my most significant achievements since last New Year?
- What were my greatest challenges since last New Year?
- What are the biggest mistakes I made since last New Year?
- What can I release from my past by forgiving myself and/or others?
- What aspect of myself would I most like to let go of in the coming year?
- What project or goal, if left undone, will I most regret next New Year?

Although the questions in Exercise 52 may appear simple on the surface, they actually provide much food for contemplation. For example, if you can identify the times when life is most meaningful for you, how often do these events occur? Could you have more of them? If so, what prevents this from happening? All in all, your answers to each question can give you plenty to think about to help you understand what's going on inside yourself at a deeper level.

Awareness

"Know thyself" is one of the most ancient instructions for those pursuing personal growth. Believe me, there are always more things we don't know about ourselves than we might think! In order to keep an eye on those areas which require help and healing, we need to develop as much awareness as possible.

- *Awareness* helps you to become conscious of your beliefs, limiting and otherwise
- *Awareness* helps you to see where you're challenged and where you succeed
- *Awareness* allows you to experience more meaning, healing and well-being on all levels of your life
- *Awareness* opens up insights about your inner potential and helps you to become who you really are

Insights appear in flashes rather like sunlight dances through leaves. Catch those glimpses of understanding by writing them down when they filter through, otherwise they may slip through your fingers! Intuitive thoughts and feelings are like seeing things out of the corner of your eye. How many times have you brushed aside an intuitive thought about something and then wished later that you hadn't? Intuition nudges us in the ribs, time after time! Don't be in such a hurry to dismiss those little pieces of perception that filter though.

Always try to keep your mind as open as possible, otherwise you may find you block out opportunities which come your way. It's easy to fall into the trap of trying to control too much and to place rigid conditions on *exactly* how you want things to happen in your life. There's nothing wrong with having a "wish list", but instead of carving it in stone, write it in the sand! That way, you let go of conditions and simply allow your desires, aims and efforts to unfold in whatever way is best for all concerned.

You see, when you can trust that what you seek will come in the form in which you *need* it and not necessarily in the form in which you *want* it, and when you're prepared to accept that it will come when you're *ready* for it and *not before that time*, you'll start finding that unexpected coincidences and signs appear in your life to give you guidance. For instance, you might find a book or a magazine article suddenly comes your way that tells you about something you need to know. Or you may discover that in seeking change, a chance meeting with a stranger may provide you with a whole set of new opportunities. The psychologist Carl Jung described these meaningful "coincidences" as synchronicities. Watch out for them, because they're important signposts which can lead you towards your personal rivers.

Winter is a time to take better care of yourself—for health reasons, if nothing else! It's always good to develop a more loving and nurturing attitude towards yourself. A lot of people have difficulty with this concept. They believe it's OK to care for and look after others, but that caring about oneself is wrong, egotistical or selfish—and probably all three!

Kindness and Compassion

I've already mentioned that we all have an inner voice that criticises who we are and what we do and is often referred to as the "Inner Critic". It's always putting us down and pulling the carpet from under our feet. Very often the Critic's voice has echoes of some parent, relative or teacher who may have lacked the ability to be encouraging and supportive in our early days. Perhaps they unwittingly brought you down with disparaging remarks such as, "You got 95% in that test? So what happened to the other 5%?"

Remarks like that can easily lead to low self esteem and a tendency towards fiercely unkind self criticism. The sad thing is that often, long after we've removed ourselves from the orbit of people who undermined us in this way, the Inner Critic takes over and continues to inflict similar damage throughout our adult life. So be aware of how much you pull yourself to pieces and try to identify whose voice is behind this practise. Recognise how unconstructive it is energetically to put yourself down so badly, and make a commitment to being kinder to yourself.

It's also good to be aware of what you're judging or criticising in the people around you as well. Like it or not—the behaviour and attitude we condemn in others is very often something we do ourselves! When something really irritates you, do yourself a favour and check out how prone you are to doing this thing yourself! Even though you may find this unthinkable, you'd be amazed at how often you're equally at fault. It's not an easy lesson to learn, but once you've accepted it, you'll be very glad that you have!

If you want to develop more kindness and compassion, not only towards yourself but also towards others, Exercise 53 outlines a wonderful 2,500-year-old Buddhist meditation practise to help you do so.

Exercise 53: Loving Kindness Meditation

Close your eyes. Come into your breath and spend a few moments focussing and centring yourself. When you're ready to begin, bring to mind some image of you holding yourself lovingly. You might try seeing yourself enfolded in a soft pink or blue aura, or imagine cradling yourself as a tiny child.

Then start repeating the following verse over and over again in your mind:

> May I be filled with loving kindness
> May I be well
> May I be peaceful and at ease
> May I be happy

Practise this regularly over a period of several weeks for good effect.

As you develop more feelings of kindness and compassion towards yourself, you might like to start extending this towards others within the same meditation period.

You could practise Loving Kindness for friends, relations, animals, or even the world in general! Do one person at a time, picture them as clearly as you can, and give each one your focus for at least 5 minutes.

All you need to do is to alter the words slightly as follows for each set of meditations:

> May he/she be filled with loving kindness
> May he/she be well
> May he/she be peaceful and at ease
> May he/she be happy

This is also a very powerful practise to do for people who are causing you problems; e.g., noisy or unco-operative neighbours, unpleasant work colleagues or others which show you animosity. Practise the Loving Kindness Meditation for them over several weeks and see how beneficial this can be in changing the nature of your relationship with such people.

Daily meditation is such a good way of developing the ability to still the mind. If you haven't already done so, turn back to Chapters 6 and 7 and try out some of the techniques I've given you. Once you've found a meditation that feels right, try to make a commitment to do it every day. And if you can't manage to do it regularly, try supplementing your practise with some quiet time as often as possible. See below for some ideas:

- Sit quietly beside a clear pond (preferably with the sunlight twinkling on it) and contemplate the light dancing on the water. It's very mesmerising.

- Enjoy watching a sunset and EmoTrance the feeling of its soft gentle energies. Review Exercise 38 (page 115), Feasting on Energy, to ensure that you really nourish yourself with its tranquillity.)

- Give yourself a break from the relentless media output of our culture. Try going without newspapers, magazines, listening to the radio or watching television for a week! You'll be surprised how much quieter your mind is after a few days.

- Or if a week seems impossibly long, try just a day of silence and mindfulness (whilst forgoing all of the above)!

- Sit in a candlelit bath and watch the flame shimmering in the bath water. Allow yourself to dwell in the quiet, still, one-pointedness of this experience. (You could also try doing the Moon Lake Reflection meditation (Exercise 19, page 56) if you're having a bath by the light of a single candle).

Dreams

As the days grow shorter and the nights become longer, it's easy to see how we're being influenced by winter. The cold weather makes many people want to sleep more, so automatically we're moving into a bit of a "hibernation" mode. I know I tend to sleep longer when it's cold and dark in the mornings. Sleeping (and dreaming) is both very beneficial to our health and well-being. The conscious mind and the body require about eight hours sleep each day, although some people are happy with less. As we age, sleep requirements may diminish to six or seven hours. Whichever category you fit into, sleep provides vital time for the body to rest and rejuvenate, and also benefits the immune system, so try to ensure that you get enough of it.

We all dream when we sleep, even those people who insist they never do! It's just that they don't remember them! There are many different types of dreams. There's Lucid Dreaming, where the dreamer actually becomes aware that they're dreaming and can direct themselves back into the dream if they wake up. They can even take control over the characters and the environment of the dream if they choose to do so.

Recurring Dreams are those where the themes of previous dreams are repeated and that re-surface in your dream state from time to time. In addition, there are nightmares where something traumatic or unpleasant is happening, or prophetic dreams which seem to predict a future event.

Many people claim to have received creative inspiration through a dream. The writer Robert Louis Stevenson is said to have been inspired to write his book about Dr Jekyll and Mr Hyde through a dream. The same thing happened with the famous Beatles song, "Yesterday". And Handel apparently heard the last part of his celebrated "The Messiah" in a dream.

Dreams are a very important part of our brain processing. Current thinking has it that dreams help us sift through the events of the day. They can also help us become aware of some hidden emotion that lies buried deep within about which we often have no awareness. So, don't dismiss your dreams— they can give an indication of what's going on in the unconscious mind.

If you'd like to get better at understanding the messages you receive from your unconscious, the best way to begin is to start keeping a dream diary and commence recording your dreams (Exercise 54).

Exercise 54: Keeping a Dream Diary

Get into the habit of writing down your dreams because they're frequently forgotten within a short time after waking. If you can manage to do this, you may notice that certain patterns are emerging over a period of time which are useful indicators of any issues, fears or anxieties you may be feeling at a very deep level.

Although recalling dreams is a perfectly natural process, it requires practise. But the more you work at it, the better you become.

Here are some things you can do to improve your dream recall.

- Before you go to sleep, ask to remember your dreams. Whisper your request out loud, or say it mentally

- Keep a notebook beside your bed specifically for dreams and make a point of writing them down as soon as you wake in the morning whilst you can still remember them. (If you leave it till later in the day, you'll probably find you've forgotten what you dreamt.)

- If you wake up in the middle of the night after a dream, just jot down a few key points to jog your memory in the morning rather than trying to write out the whole experience. (Writing an account of the dream there and then could end up making you too wide awake and prevent you from getting back to sleep again.)

- Write down everything you can remember—characters, images, locations etc. You'll find the more you write, the more you remember.

- Sometimes you'll remember more of a dream later in the day because something triggers recall—a person, an event or whatever. Again, try to write it down or make some brief notes as soon as you remember it.

Writing out dreams is a really good way to increase your intuition because dreams and intuition are very closely related.

The subject of dream interpretation is something that has fascinated the human race for thousands of years. The ancient Greeks worked with dreams for healing purposes and also saw them as a means to receive divine advice and prophecies. Other ancient civilisations have also relied heavily upon them as a means of guidance and inspiration. The Native Americans devised ways of inducing a prophetic dream called a Vision Quest by fasting and praying until a dream came to them which would guide them forward in their lives.

Dream interpretation came to the fore in the West in the early 20th century through the work of the psychologist, Sigmund Freud, and psychiatrist, Carl Jung, both of whom believed that dreaming was an interaction between the conscious and unconscious mind. Marie Louise von Franz, who worked closely with Jung, said, "Dreams generally point to our blind spot. They never tell us what we already know. They will tell us what we don't know."*

Recent research has shown that the main emotion to surface in dreams is anxiety as well as pain and fears of abandonment. Negative emotions appear to be felt more regularly than positive ones.

Personally, I've found the most satisfactory way of interpreting dreams is to work on the understanding that every person you dream about is a symbol of some aspect of yourself. This applies no matter whether the "characters" in your dream are male or female. You see, we all have male and female within us. In very basic terms, anything to do with nurturing, receiving, caring, healing, being creative, intuitive or perceptive, is about the feminine aspect of ourselves. Whilst on the other hand, the parts of us which plan, assess, build, fix and construct, are to do with putting things out in the world and are all aspects of our masculine side. This means that dreaming about a man or a woman—whether you know them or not—can signify the male or female sides of our personalities, and aren't necessarily who or what they appear to be. It's therefore important to take note of what those figures are doing and saying in your dreams as it will apply to some aspect of your life.

Don't take your dreams literally. Remember, everything you experience in dreams is symbolic. A dream about death and dying for example can simply signal that you're moving into a new phase in your life and letting go of some old baggage.

Working with your dreams can be both healing and a tremendous source of guidance and wisdom. As Denise Linn says, "…(They can) foretell your future, reveal your past, and warn you of danger. They can contain creative inspiration or assist in releasing the barriers of your life. Dreams can serve as a doorway to a mystic arena for inner-dimensional travel and communication with loved ones who have passed on. They can be a springboard for night healing, astral travel, and soul searching."†

---

* From *The Way of the Dream* by Marie Louise von Franz.
† From *The Hidden Power of Dreams* by Denise Linn.

Unfortunately, there isn't space in this book to go deeply into the subject of interpretation or other ways of working with your dreams. However, if you want to find out more about dreams and how to interpret them, there are lots of fascinating books on this subject, some of which are listed at the back of the book in the Further Information and Suggested Reading section.

Winter on an Inner Level

From the beginning of Spring, Nature leads us in the direction of activity and growth. But after reaping the fruits of all her efforts in the autumn, she's clearly no longer generating the high levels of energy that we saw in previous months. This change is often reflected in our personal energy at this time of year and we may become aware of tiring more easily. As winter draws in, there's a sense of slowing down, of not wanting to do some of the things we usually do, of accomplishing less, and sometimes feeling that we don't know anything. We may go through patches of believing that nothing's happening and life may seem a bit dull. It's often a time that gives rise to a sense of having undone the benefits of all the efforts we made previously, a time when we may lose heart, forget our courage and strength, or feel sad and lonely or empty.

When and if this happens, we're simply experiencing the darkness that comes before the light. This is a time when we sometimes enter into the mysterious and shadowy unknown where it's hard to see and we're no longer certain of where we are. Familiar objects assume strange shapes in the gloom making it difficult to find our bearings, and this is the season when we may struggle to hold our balance and feel the security of the earth beneath our feet.

Winter is a period of gestation—of waiting in the darkness before moving forwards into the light. And it helps to remember that however uncomfortable and scary this might feel, there's a very positive side to it. When things are shrouded in darkness, we no longer see their separateness, for they all merge into one. So, if you feel you're wandering around in a shadowy winter landscape and not seeing the wood for the trees, what's actually happening is that you're going through a period of integration. It's as if you need to lose your way before you find a better route. You need to feel a sense of loss before you realise how much you have. By embracing the darkness in yourself (i.e., those parts of you which need help and healing), you have the chance of becoming more whole, more connected, and closer to your true nature.

When life gets uncomfortable and you're afraid you're losing your way, remember there are always things you can do to get back on track and out of the densest part of the jungle. Just remember what you've learnt! And try some of the following:

- When things get tough and you're feeling that low winter energy, try using Exercise 37 (page 114), Evoking Innocent Energy. It's such a lovely gentle healing to give yourself.

- If you need spiritual uplift, try Exercise 18 (page 54), Uplifting and Unburdening the Heart. It's a really beautiful, transformational meditation.

- Go back to Exercise 2 (page 5), and take refuge in your safe place

- Keep Journaling! Get it all down on the page! It's better out than in!! You can track your progress this way, too.

- EFT or EmoTrance your distress (see Chapters 12 and 13).

Celebrate Winter

There's no doubt that the period around Winter Solstice, which is one of the oldest celebrations in the world, is a magical and very special time with all the customs which we still continue of connecting with family and friends, singing and feasting. What better way, then, to end the final chapter of this book than with a Winter Solstice Ritual you might like to perform for yourself! Don't forget, you need to check the date of the Solstice as it changes from year to year.

This is definitely another ritual where you could invite like-minded friends to come round and join you. Solstice is a time for being with loved ones, enjoying their company and giving gifts. It's also a time of feasting and merriment, so get ready for a party afterwards! Prepare some food and ask those coming to bring edible contributions. Also have a tray of glasses and some bottles of wine or juice ready to drink after the ritual (Exercise 55).

Exercise 55: Winter Solstice: The Return of the Sun

Spread cloths of green, red and white on your altar and choose candles of the same colours. Add in some holly, ivy, and pine cones, etc.

Make or buy wreaths of holly and ivy. Place one on or near your altar and maybe hang another on your front door. If you like Christmas trees, then by all means have one in your home and make sure it's decorated by the time Solstice arrives. Hang up strings of those little white fairy lights you can buy and have them trailing across the mantelpieces, winding through banisters, or strung across doorways and over mirrors. Have fun being creative and decorate your home with a happy, childish sense of play.

Find a wide, shallow bowl suitable for displaying floating candles and fill it with water. Have enough floating candles for each person who is coming to join you for the ritual and put them in a container. Buy a packet of Christmas glitter or some of those little metallic gold or silver stars which are fun to scatter on surfaces. Keep these items all together and set them aside for the moment.

Before people arrive, set out the food and light your ordinary candles (not the floaters). Switch on the fairy lights and light some incense or joss sticks. Place your floating candle bowl on or by your altar. Open the packet of glitter and scatter some over the water, or throw in some of the stars so that when the floating candles are lit, you get a reflected twinkle from them.

If people are bringing presents, ask them to put them under the tree or by the altar before sitting down in a circle. Once everyone has arrived and settled, you can begin.

Turn out all the lights and blow out all the candles, but keep one beside you together with some matchsticks and a saucer for the dead matches.

Close your eyes and start following your breath. When you feel ready, take yourself (if you're doing this on your own) or lead the others into the following guided meditation.

Visualise being outside in the dark. Imagine a tree (it may be one in your own garden, if you have one) with its bare branches silhouetted against a moonlit sky. Look up at its crown and then let your eyes travel downwards, along its trunk and down towards its roots. Imagine following them down deep into the earth below and being able to see what's happening underneath the soil. See how the tree roots mingle with the roots of other trees and those of nearby plants and bushes. See all the spring bulbs buried there with small healthy little shoots emerging from them. You can also see tiny stems peeping out from the roots of other plants. All are moving slowly upwards towards the surface of the earth with great intention. Stay with this image for a few moments and take inspiration from all this hidden activity.

Now, withdraw your attention from the earth and imagine again that you're looking at the tree with its bare branches and the general sparseness of vegetation around it. Spend a little while with this image, knowing that despite the apparent barrenness on the surface of the earth, Nature is carrying new life in her womb. And so it is for you—metaphorically. New things are in the process of growing towards the time of birth. Despite the darkness, we still grow, and fresh insights, perspectives and understandings will come with the return of the light in spring. Stay with this idea for a few moments more, and then slowly come back into the room.

Light the candle beside you and then get up and bring the bowl of water down from the altar and place it in the centre of the circle. Put the container of floating candles beside it as well as the matches and the saucer. Invite your friends to celebrate the return of the Sun by each taking a floating candle in turn, floating it on the water and saying what they'd like the light to bring into the world (i.e., peace, generosity, compassion, understanding, truth, etc.) Enjoy the blaze of the little lights as they grow in number and the twinkle of stars beneath the water or the glitter dust on its surface.

Ask everyone to join hands in the circle and give thanks for the priceless gifts of friendship and love, the joy and magic of the season and the promise of things to come. If you like, you could then all sing (to the tune of *We Wish You a Merry Christmas*) "We wish you a Merry Solstice, We wish you a Merry Solstice, We wish you a Merry Solstice, and a Happy New Year!"

Then light all the other candles and switch on the fairy lights. Pour out the wine or juice or whatever, and invite everyone to drink a toast to the returning Sun and all that it means for each person. Then distribute the presents and enjoy the party!

This is my suggestion for celebrating the Winter Solstice, but feel free to be creative and do your own thing.

Wishing you peace, light,
happiness, abundance and fulfilment
throughout every season!

Finding the River

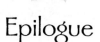

Epilogue

I've never written a book before, and I have to say that in the beginning, the task felt more than a little daunting. I definitely got lost in the jungle and took some wrong turnings before I found the stream that led me in the right direction!

EFT and EmoTrance came to the rescue and got me through several attacks of writer's block. Other first aid techniques included liberal doses of Reiki (both received and self administered), not to mention pacing myself, meditating and generally walking my talk! I'm also much indebted to the skillful encouragement of my mentor, Silvia Hartmann, to whom I'm eternally grateful for helping me to complete such a major undertaking.

In the process of writing, I was continually reminded of how much we can learn from Nature's ability to adapt herself to upheavals, obstacles and difficulties. Her tenacity and flexibility provides an inspirational example of how to survive and continue to grow even in adversity. My first spiritual and personal growth teacher was always saying, "When things get bad, remember how plants can grow through concrete!" I've never forgotten that, and his words still echo in my mind when the going gets tough.

It's very easy to lose sight of what we can do to help ourselves when the mind is solid with too many thoughts or anxieties. We can so easily slide into mental swings and roundabouts and spiral down into pain or negativity, or reach a point of exhaustion and overwhelm. I hope so much that this book helps you to understand that there's always a way through these things, that we don't have to become "victims" and that there's so much more we can do to help and heal ourselves than we might imagine.

We're all energetic beings living in an energetic world with a powerful connection between mind, body and spirit. We're multi-levelled creatures with physical, mental, emotional and spiritual aspects to us, and our personal and spiritual development encompasses *all* of these levels. The aim of *Finding the River* is to start recognising and working with that energy, integrating the scattered parts of ourselves, acknowledging our uniqueness, and flowing with our potential.

If you're just beginning your journey of healing and self-discovery, I hope you find that the things I've taught you in this book inspire you to take your first steps. If you're already on your way, my wish is that it encourages you to adventure farther afield and embrace new ideas and techniques. And if you've been travelling for some time, I really hope it supports you on every level as you tread the path towards discovering who you really are.

With love and blessings

Sally

September 2009

www.energyharmonix.co.uk

Further Information
and Suggested Reading

Prologue

Documentary films about Juliane Koepke's crash survival.

Miracoli Accadono Ancora (Miracles Still Happen). 1974. Giuseppe Maria Scotese. Based on the true story of Juliane Koepke's ordeal in the Amazonian jungle.

Wings of Hope. Documentary film made in 2000 by Werner Herzog in which Juliane Koepke herself takes part, revisits the crash site and talks about how she managed to survive.

Chapter 1

The Endorphin Effect. William Bloom (www.williambloom.com).

Feeling Safe. William Bloom.

Soul-ution: The Holistic Manifesto. William Bloom.

The Foundation for Holistic Spirituality (www.f4hs.org).

Chapter 2

The Endorphin Effect. William Bloom (www.williambloom.com).

The Genie in Your Genes. Dawson Church (www.genieinyourgenes.com).

The Biology of Belief. Bruce Lipton (www.brucelipton.com).

Molecules of Emotion. Candace B. Pert (www.candacepert.com).

Chapter 3

The Mind–Body Bible. Dr Mark Atkinson (www.drmarkatkinson.com).

Creating Health: How To Wake Up the Body's Intelligence. Deepak Chopra (www.deepakchopra.com).

The Chopra Centre (www.chopra.com).

Anatomy of an Illness. Norman Cousins.

Staying Healthy with the Seasons. Elson M Haas (www.elsonhaas.com).

The New Detox Diet. Elson M Haas.

Optimum Nutrition Made Easy. Patrick Holford (www.patrickholford.com).

The Amazing Liver and Gall Bladder Flush. Andreas Moritz (www.ener-chi.com).

The Creation of Health: The Emotional, Psychological and Spiritual Responses that Promote Health and Healing. Caroline Myss.

Why People Don't Heal and How They Can. Caroline Myss.

Caroline Myss Institute (www.myss.com).

Your Body Speaks Your Mind. Deb Shapiro (www.edanddebshapiro.com).

The English Federation of Disability Sport (www.wheelpower.org.ukl).

Chapter 4

The Endorphin Effect. William Bloom (www.williambloom.com).

The Artist's Way. Julia Cameron (www.theartistsway.com).

Chris James (www.chrisjames.net)

Jill Purce (www.jillpurce.com).

Singing for the Brain (www.alzheimers.org.uk).

Chapter 5

The Relaxation and Stress Reduction Workbook. Martha Davis, Elizabeth Robbins and Matthew McKay.

Stress Relief and Relaxation Techniques. Judith Lazarus.

The 20-Minute Break. Ernest Lawrence Rossi PhD (www.ernestrossi.com).

A Discourse with Our Genes. Ernest Lawrence Rossi.

Dreams, Consciousness, and Spirit. Ernest Lawrence Rossi.

Mind–Body Therapy. Ernest Lawrence Rossi.

Chapter 6

Books on Meditation

Journey of Awakening: A Meditator's Guidebook. Ram Dass (www.ramdass.org).

Peace is Every Step. Thich Nhat Hahn (www.interbeing.org.uk).

Breathe! You are Alive! Thich Nhat Hahn.

Walking Meditation (Book, CD and DVD). Thich Nhat Hahn.

The Book of Meditation. Chris Jarmey

How to Meditate. Lawrence LeShan (www.spiritsite.com).

Meditation is... Bodel Rikys (www.zedweb.co.uk).

The Meditation Bible: The Definitive Guide to Meditation. Jane Struthers

Wherever You Go, There You Are. Jon Kabat-Zin (www.mindfulnesstapes.com).

Meditation Centres (see also Spiritual Centres under Chapter 7)

ACEM International School of Meditation (www.acem.com) (Non-Religious Meditation).

Plum Village Meditation Practice Centre (www.plumvillage.org). Headquarters of renowned Zen Buddhist monk Thich Nhat Hahn.

Transcendental Meditation (www.t-m.org.uk) (International Meditation School with around 40 centres in UK teaching simple meditation technique based in Indian Tradition.

Tai Chi and Chi Kung

For classes in your area, consult local directories

Books on Chi Kung and Tai Chi:

Chi Kung. Master Lam Kam Chuen (www.lamassociation.com).

Tai Chi. Peter Chin Kean Choy (www.rainbow-taichi.org.uk).

Chapter 7

Books on Spirituality

Fire in the Heart: A Spiritual Guide for Teens. Deepak Chopra (www.chopra.com).

How Long is Now? How to be Spiritually Aware in the Real World. Tim Freke (www.timothyfreke.com).

The Direct Path. Andrew Harvey (www.andrewharvey.net)

The Hope: A Guide to Sacred Activism. Andrew Harvey.

A New Earth. Eckhart Tolle (www.eckharttolle.com).

The Power of Now. Eckhart Tolle.

The Search for Spirituality. Ursula King (www.spiritualityandpractise.com).

A Path with Heart. Jack Kornfield (www.jackkornfield.org).

Seeking the Heart of Wisdom. Jack Kornfield

The Road Less Travelled. M Scott Peck—www.mscottpeck.com

Conversations with God. Neale Donald Walsch (www.nealedonaldwalsch.com).

Spiritual Centres

British Taoist Association (www.taoists.co.uk)
   Taoist Teachings—Eastern philosophical and religious tradition.

Buddhist Centres in the UK (www.chezpaul.org.uk).

International Centres for Mindfulness (www.jackkornfield.com
   Buddhist Mindfulness Meditation.

Kabbalah: (www.Kabbalah.com)
   International Centres for Learning Judaic-based spiritual teachings.

Radha Soami Spiritual Path (also known as Sant Mat): (www.radha-soami.info)
   Sikh-based method of God realisation.

Siddha Yoga (www.syduk.org)
   Hindu-based spiritual path.

Sufi Teachings: (www.schoolofsufiteaching.org) (www.sufiorderuk.org)
   Esoteric arm of Islam.

Thich Nhat Hanh UK & International Sanghas (www.interbeing.org.uk) Zen
   Buddhist Centres focussed on the teachings of Thich Nhat Hahn.

Zen Buddhism (www.iriz.hanazono.ac.jp)
   List of International Zen Buddhist Centres.

Alternatives—St James's Church, Piccadilly, London Tel: 020 7287 6711:
   (admin@alternatives.org.uk www.alternatives.org.uk)

Hosts Monday night talks on spirituality, creativity and wellbeing by some of the best known names in the mind–body–spirit world.

Chapter 8

The Body Electric. Robert Becker.

The Tao of Physics. Fritjof Capra (www.fritjofcapra.net).

Perfect Health. Deepak Chopra (www.chopra.com).

Vibrational Medicine. Richard Gerber M.D.

Chakra Balancing. Anodea Judith (www.sacredcenters.com).

Ayurveda: The Science of Self-Healing. Dr Vasant Lad (www.ayurveda.com).

The Field: The Quest for the Secret Force of the Universe. Lynne McTaggart (www.livingthefield.ning.com).

The Sun and the Serpent. Hamish Miller and Paul Broadhurst.

Chi: Discovering Your Life Energy. Master Waysun Liao (www.taichiaocenter.com).

Advanced Energy Anatomy. Caroline Myss (Audio CD) (www.myss.com).

Anatomy of the Spirit. Caroline Myss.

Energy Anatomy: The Science of Personal Power, Spirituality and Health. Caroline Myss (Audio CD).

The Dancing Wu Li Masters. Gary Zukav (www.zukav.com).

Chapter 9

Clear Your Clutter with Feng Shui. Karen Kingston (www.spaceclearing.com)

Sacred Space. Denise Linn (www.deniselinn.com).

Clearing Clutter Choices. Barbara Tako (www.clutterclearingchoices.com).

How to De-Junk Your Life. Dawna Walters and Mark Franks.

Organized Living: Clutter-Clearing Strategies and Creative Storage Solutions. Dawna Walters.

Herbal Colon Cleanse: Specialist Herbal Supplies For Practitioners (www.shs100.com).

Feng Shui Organisations and Practitioner Listings

Association of UK Feng Shui (www.webring.com).

The Feng Shui Society (www.fengshuisociety.org.uk).

The Feng Shui Agency (www.fengshuiagency.com).

Chapter 10

Books

The Feng Shui Bible: The Definitive Guide to Practising Feng Shui. Simon Brown.

Clear Your Clutter. Karen Kingston (www.spaceclearing.com).

Creating Sacred Space with Feng Shui. Karen Kingston.

The Feng Shui House Book. Gina Lazenby (www.thehealthyhome.com).

Feng Shui for the Soul. Denise Linn (www.deniselinn.com).

Sacred Space. Denise Linn.

Bells:

www.spaceclearing.com

Feng Shui Suppliers

The Feng Shui Company (www.fengshuisite.com)

Incense Burners, Charcoal and Incense

www.bombayincense.com

www.watkinsbooks.com

Rattles and Drums:

www.bongocentral.com

www.livingdrums.com

Resin Incense and Charcoal Tablets

www.bombayincense.com)

www.prinknashabbey.org

www.watkinsbooks.com

Tibetan Bells

www.GarudaTrading.com

www.watkinsbooks.com

Music

New World Music (www.newworldmusic.com).

Mysteries (www.mysteries.co.uk).

Tibetan Bells Music—Nada Himalya. Deuter (www.newearthrecords.com).

www.watkinsbooks.com)

Bach Flower Remedies

www.bachshop.co.uk

Space Clearing Mist

www.ausflowers.com.au

Chapter 11

Books on Energy Medicine

Energy Medicine. Donna Eden with David Feinstein (www.innersource.net).

Energy Medicine Essential Techniques. Donna Eden (DVD).

Energy Medicine for Women. Donna Eden with David Feinstein.

The Energy Medicine Kit. Donna Eden.

Energy Medicine: The Scientific Basis. James L Oschman
 (www.energyresearch.bizland.com).

Energy Umbrella Organisations and Practitioner Listings

Acupuncture (www.acupuncture.org.uk).

Applied Kinesiology (www.appliedkinesiology.com).

Polarity Therapy (www.ukpta.org.uk).

Reflexology (www.aor.org.uk).

Reiki (www.reikifed.co.uk).

Shiatsu (www.shiatsu.org).

Therapeutic Touch (www.ttouch.org.uk).

Chapter 12

Books on EmoTrance

Energy Magic: The Patterns and Techniques of EmoTrance, Vol 3. Silvia Hartmann
 (www.silviahartmann.com).

Living Energy: The Patterns and Techniques of EmoTrance, Vol 2. Silvia Hartmann.

Oceans of Energy: The Patterns and Techniques of EmoTrance, Vol 1. Silvia Hartmann.

The Love Clinic. Sandra Hilawi (www.passionforhealth.com).

For Books, CDs, Events and Practitioner Listings

EmoTrance (www.emotrance.com).

For eTraining Manuals and Distance Learning

Sidereus Foundation (www.sidereus.org).

Chapter 13

Books on EFT

The Healing Power of EFT and Energy Psychology. David Feinstein, Donna Eden and
 Gary Craig (www.innersource.net).

EFT for Dummies. Helen Fone.

EFT in Your Pocket: Tapping into Emotional Freedom. Isy Grigg (www.eft4me.com).

Advanced Patterns of EFT. Silvia Hartmann (www.silviahartmann.com).

Adventures in EFT. Silvia Hartmann.

Emotional Healing in Minutes. Valerie and Paul Lynch (www.friendsinfocus.co.uk).

Tapping for Kids. Angie Mucillo (www.TappingForKids.wordpress.com).

Art and Science of Emotional Freedom, The. Ananga Sivyer (www.ananga.net).

Gary Craig's Website (www.emofree.com).

For EFT Practitioner Listings, Courses, Trainings, and Manuals

The Association for Meridian Energy Therapies (www.theamt.com).

Chapter 14

The Seven Spiritual Laws of Success. Deepak Chopra (www.chopra.com).

The Power of Intention. Dr Wayne Dwyer www.drwaynedwyer.com).

The New De-Tox Diet. Elson M. Haas and Daniella Chase (www.elsonhaas.com).

The Intention Experiment. Lynne McTaggart www.theintentionexperiment.com).

Detox For Life. Carol Vorderman.

The Detox Cook. Louisa J Walters, Aliza Baron Cohen and Adrian Mercuri.

For Equinox dates (www.en.wikipedia.org/wiki/Equinox)

Chapter 15

The Secret. Rhonda Byrne (www.thesecret.tv).

Love as a Way of Life. Gary Chapman (www.garychapman.org).

Overcoming Low Self-Esteem. Dr Melanie Fennell.

Men Are From Mars Women Are From Venus. John Gray
    (www.home.marsvenus.com).

Love Yourself, Heal Your Life Workbook. Louise L Hay (www.louisehay.com).

You Can Heal Your Life. Louise Hay.

Ask and it is Given. Esther and Jerry Hicks (www.abraham-hicks.com).

Abundance through Reiki. Paula Horan (www.healyourselfwithoxygen.com).

Attracting Abundance with EFT. Carol Look (www.attractingabundance.com).

The Cosmic Ordering Service. Baerbel Mohr (www.baerbelmohr.de).

I Deserve Love. Sondra Ray (www.sondraray.com).

The Loving Relationships Treasury. Sondra Ray.

For Solstice dates (www.en.wikipedia.org/wiki/Solstice)

Chapter 16

The First 30 Days: Making Any Change Easier. Ariane de Bonvoisin
    (www.first30days.com).

Change Your Thoughts, Change Your Life. Dr Wayne W Dyer
    (www.drwaynedwyer.com).

Gratitude: A Way of Life. Louise L Hay (www.louisehay.com).

How to Want What You Have. Timothy Miller (dr.timothymiller.com).

Meister Eckhart: From Whom God Hid Nothing. David O'Neal.

Attitudes of Gratitude: How to Give and Receive Joy Everyday of Your Life. MJ Ryan
    (www.mj-ryan.com).

*Authentic Happiness: Using the New Positive Psychology to Realise Your Potential for
    Lasting Fulfillment.* Martin EP Seligman (www.authentichappiness.sas).

Learned Optimism: How to Change Your Mind and Your Life. Martin EP Seligman.

Gift of Change, The: Spiritual Guidance for a Radically New Life. Marianne Williamson (www.marianne.com).

Chapter 17

Synchrodestiny: Harnessing the Infinite Power of Coincidence to Create Miracles. Deepak Chopra (www.chopra.com).

The Spontaneous Fulfillment of Desire. Deepak Chopra.

The Way of the Dream. Marie Louise von Franz.

The Art of Forgiveness, Loving Kindness and Peace. Jack Kornfield (www.jackkornfield.org).

The Hidden Power of Dreams. Denise Linn (www.deniselinn.com).

The Dream Bible: The Definite Guide to Over 300 Dream Symbols. Brenda Mallon.

About the Author

Originally trained as an actress, Sally spent a number of years working professionally in regional theatre, as well as radio, film and television. Her interest in alternative therapy and personal and spiritual development ran in tandem with her theatrical career and gradually led her towards a personal journey of self-discovery.

Sally has explored many paths and techniques over the years in her quest for healing and spiritual unfolding under the direction of a number of highly skilled therapists, trainers and spiritual teachers. She has studied Astrology, Dowsing, Energy Medicine, Feng Shui, Transpersonal Psychology, Jungian Dream Interpretation and Cognitive Analytic Therapy. She has also done courses in spiritual care under the auspices of RIGPA (The Tibetan Buddhist Centre). In addition she spent six years following the Sikh tradition of Sant Mat under the guidance of Maharaj Charan Singh and later studied the Hindu path of Siddha Yoga and the teachings of Mother Meera before synthesising this wealth of wisdom into a personal spiritual practice which she has continued ever since. She has also completed a three-year study course in Holistic and Spiritual Growth with Dr William Bloom.

She is qualified as a Reiki Master/Practitioner, an Advanced EFT Practitioner, an EmoTrance Practitioner, an Endorphin Technique Practitioner, and has a private practice in North West London. She also teaches meditation to beginners.

Sally is passionate about the work she does, deeply interested in the people she is privileged to work with and committed to using her healing skills with integrity.

To learn more about Energy Therapy, please visit Sally at
www.energyharmonix.co.uk

Finding the River